MW01076144

Ara'

c'

Goo ne ' O⁻ x +

ROCK IN A HARD PLACE

FEATURING

al-Namrood

Ambrotype

Ayat

Bathory

Blaakyum

Black Sabbath

Breeze of the Dying

Burzum

Cannibal Corpse

Chaos of Nazareth

Confess

Creative Waste

DAM

Damaar

Dark Philosophy

Darkthrone

Dawn of Rage

Dead Kennedys

Deicide

Detox

Dimmu Borgir

Eminem

Emperor

Equation

Erfan Paydar

Eslam Jawaad

From the Vastland

Gorgoroth

Grieving Age

Guns N' Roses

Hatecrowned

Immortal

Judas Priest

Katatonia

Khalas

Korn

Kurt Cobain

Lamb of God

Lydia Canaan

Malikah

Marilyn Manson

Massive Scar Era

Master of Persia

Mayhem

Melechesh

Metallica

N.W.A.

Nader Sadek

Napalm Death

Nasum

Nekhei Na'atza

Nightchains

Nirvana

Opeth

Orchid

Orion

Palestinian Rapperz

Ramy Essam

Refugees of Rap

Scarab

Sepultura

Sheikh Imam

Slayer

Soap Kills

Sorg Innkalleise

Sound of Ruby

System Ali

Tamer Nafar

The Free Keys

The New

Government

Tupac Shakur

Useless ID

Venom

Wasted Land

x-Beyond East

Yellow Dogs

Ziad and the Wings

ROCK IN A HARD PLACE

MUSIC AND MAYHEM IN THE MIDDLE EAST

ORLANDO CROWCROFT

ZED

Zed Books

LONDON

Rock in a Hard Place: Music and Mayhem in the Middle East was first published in 2017 by Zed Books Ltd, The Foundry, 17 Oval Way, London SE11 5RR, UK.

www.zedbooks.net

Copyright © Orlando Crowcroft 2017

The right of Orlando Crowcroft to be identified as the author of this work has been asserted by him in accordance with the Copyright, Designs and Patents Act 1988.

Typeset in Haarlemmer by seagulls.net
Cover design by Clare Turner
Cover photo © George Durzi/Jorzine, www.georgedurziphotography.com

All rights reserved. No part of this publication may be reproduced, stored in a retrieval system or transmitted in any form or by any means, electronic, mechanical, photocopying or otherwise, without the prior permission of Zed Books Ltd.

A catalogue record for this book is available from the British Library.

ISBN 978-1-78699-016-7 hb
ISBN 978-1-78699-015-0 pb
ISBN 978-1-78699-018-1 pdf
ISBN 978-1-78699-017-4 epub
ISBN 978-1-78699-019-8 mobi

MIX
Paper from
responsible sources
FSC® C013604
www.fsc.org

Printed and bound by CPI Group (UK) Ltd, Croydon, CR0 4YY

For Helen

CONTENTS

THE MIDDLE EAST

INTRODUCTION

LIFE IS OURS, WE LIVE IT OUR WAY

--METALLICA, 'NOTHING ELSE MATTERS'

The smell of cigarettes and sweat mixed with the dust of the desert night. Hands gripping plastic glasses of weak lager, still just about cold. Bodies crammed together, a heaving mass of people, dressed mostly in black. Early arrivals are pressed up tight against slanted steel barriers. Headbangers, restless with anticipation, are behind them, Further back the crowd thins out, but not by much. It stretches way out into the night, right to the back of the Yas Arena.

Then the music blaring from the two-storey-high speakers at either side of the stage stops and the boisterous talk of the crowd is gradually replaced by a murmur. The time has come. A guttural growl rises up from somewhere like a battle cry. That tingle builds behind your rib cage, moves up your neck. You shift onto the balls of your feet to get a better look at the stage. *Where are they?* Fists are made, index and little fingers extended and then raised. The devil horns mean heavy metal wherever you are.

More and more come up and are raised above heads and between flags: Egyptian, Palestinian, Libyan, Lebanese. A roar sweeps over the crowd and at its deafening crescendo Metallica stride onto the stage like giants, silhouetted against the bright white lights. Distortion bursts from a wall of monitors and, like the first chaotic moments of a bar fight, it begins.

As I write these words five years later, I feel it all again. That rush. There are those who get it from surfing waves, others from throwing themselves out of planes, but for me it is that moment at the very beginning of a set when the music turns from noise and confusion into something you suddenly recognise: a song, or a riff. It picks you up and it carries you along. You rise and fall with it. You get beaten and bruised and covered in beer and when it is over you feel reborn.

Metallica's set that night was a blur then as it is now. I don't remember exactly what they played. I don't remember whether James Hetfield's vocals or Kirk Hammett's solos were note-perfect. But what I do remember is the crowd, 30,000-strong, from every corner of the Middle East.

I must have seen a thousand shows over the last two decades. I've seen bands play everywhere from the dingiest London squat to Wembley Arena. I've seen bands I've never heard of and bands whose songs are branded on my heart. But I have never seen anything like the show on 25 October 2011. Kirk Hammett, recalling the show a year later, told

UAE newspaper *Gulf News* that even he – who has toured the world – had been taken aback by the atmosphere: "Once we got to Abu Dhabi, we realised that we were playing to a fan base that was untapped – there were people from Lebanon, people there from Iraq, people from Iran … from all over the Middle East. Places we'd never expected we'd go to – ever." And this was a band that was used to breaking boundaries. Almost exactly 20 years before the show in Abu Dhabi, Metallica had played in Moscow, at the beginning of the opening up of the former Soviet Union and, reputedly, at the personal request of Russian leader Mikhail Gorbachev.

Metallica came to Abu Dhabi at no less of a pivotal time. In 2011, the Middle East was ablaze. In Egypt, Tahrir Square was occupied by protesters ahead of elections planned for November, the country's first since the February revolution which overthrew a dictator and captivated the world. Six days earlier, in Libya, Muammar Gaddafi had been beaten to death by rebels outside Sirte, bringing to an end 42 years of despotic rule. In Syria, the revolution had already begun its slide into armed insurgency but not yet civil war. Tunisia was basking in the glow of the uprising that ousted Zine el-Abidine Ben Ali after 23 years.

On the streets of Cairo and Tunis, Tripoli and Homs, Arabs had risen up against violence and dictatorship and achieved things that only a year earlier would have been thought impossible. Their spirit had gripped us all, wherever we were from. There was a feeling that a door had been opened, a dam had been breached, and that whatever the Arab Spring went on to become, the Middle East would never be the same again. Its spirit hung in the air that night in Abu Dhabi – victory, vision, rebellion, revolution – it surged through the crowd. It gave the show a momentum that felt utterly unstoppable, and every one of us felt it.

Metallica had brought together not just the children of those revolutions but their brothers and sisters from Saudi Arabia and Iran, Lebanon and Palestine. They brought together Shia, Sunni, Christians, Druze and atheists. They brought together young people and old people, expats and locals. All of us united in sweat and noise and song.

* * *

There is a scene in the cult 1999 film *Detroit Rock City* when a fictional group named the Mothers Against the Music of Kiss picket a concert in Detroit by the 1970s stadium rock band. The protesters, who typify buttoned-down, conservative American parents, hold signs and placards that claim that Kiss is an abbreviation of Knights in Satan's Service. The film is a comedy but the claims are steeped in fact. Gene Simmons, in his 2001 autobiography *Kiss and Make-up*, addressed them. "When I was asked whether I worshipped the devil I simply refused to answer the question for a number of reasons. The first reason, of course, was that it was good press. Let people wonder. The second was my complete disregard for the people who were asking."

As long as it has been around, heavy metal has caused controversy. In 1990, Judas Priest and their label, CBS Records, went on trial in Reno, Nevada, charged with driving two young men, Raymond Belknap and James Vance, to suicide. The pair had been drinking, smoking marijuana and listening to Judas Priest before agreeing to a suicide pact, walking to a church playground and taking it in turns to shoot themselves with a 12-gauge shotgun.

Belknap, 18, was killed instantly but Vance survived, dying three years later. The lawyers for the parents alleged that the British heavy metal band had placed subliminal messages in several of their songs. Although they were cleared, Judas Priest were in court every day for a month defending themselves against the allegations.

A decade later, heavy metal star Marilyn Manson was blamed for the 1999 Columbine High School massacre. He later wrote for *Rolling Stone*: "When it comes down to who's to blame for the high school murders in Littleton, Colorado, throw a rock and you'll hit someone who's guilty. Deep down, most adults hate people who go against the grain."

As rock music spread outside the US and Europe in the 1960s, it immediately began to raise eyebrows. In the 1960s, it was banned from Japanese television and denounced in South Korea and Greece. The former USSR was hostile to rock and later heavy metal largely because of its association with the West. Yet when Metallica played in Moscow in 1991, as many as 1.6 million people turned up. The footage of that show has entered heavy metal history: long-haired Russian youths headbanging as nervous Soviet soldiers stand guard, occasionally wading in with their clubs.

There was rock music in the Middle East as far back as the 1950s, with events such as the Baalbeck International Festival being held amongst the Roman ruins in Lebanon's Bekaa Valley. In the 1960s and 1970s, as bands such as Deep Purple and The Rolling Stones became superstars in the West, they also gained a following in Beirut and Cairo, Damascus and Baghdad. Tehran was a veritable hub for international rock bands as well as having one of the most diverse and influential local music scenes in the Middle East, if not the world, until Iran's Islamic revolution in 1979.

By the 1980s, legendary Syrian singer Jack Power – who is still living in Aleppo to this day – was performing Black Sabbath to thousands of fans in Damascus. Lydia Canaan, the first female rock star in the Middle East, was doing the same in Beirut as frontwoman of Lebanese band Equation. Lebanon had begun its slide into war and Egypt and Syria were languishing under dictatorial regimes, but it was common for Lebanese, Syrian and Egyptian radio stations to play American and European rock music. With the onset of satellite television, young Arabs had access to a multitude of western TV channels and – like the rest of us – were swept up in the tide of stadium rock and grunge, from Guns N' Roses to Nirvana.

Across the world, the 1980s saw the birth of two very different but equally controversial genres that would both go on to have a significant influence in the Middle East – and are the subject of this book.

The first was so-called 'extreme metal', which would grow out of the broader heavy metal movement and lead to subgenres including death, black, grindcore, thrash and doom. In his book *Extreme Metal: Music and Culture on the Edge*, Keith Kahn-Harris attributes this shift to the fact that, while earlier heavy metal bands drew their influence from rhythm and blues, rock and roll and other genres, extreme metal was created out of metal itself. It became harsher, less accessible and more niche.

In the UK, heavy metal became fused with punk rock and helped create bands like Venom, whose 1982 album *Black Metal* gave a new genre its name. In Norway and Sweden, it became a phenomenon, with bands such as Mayhem, Bathory and Burzum. To this day, Norway and Sweden are two of a handful of countries where black and death metal bands have vast mainstream success and are treated like celebrities.

Early in the 1990s, cassettes and CDs of these bands started appearing in the Middle East, often brought back by people who had travelled abroad. In Cairo and Tehran, young men and women started swapping tapes of Metallica and Slayer and so the Middle East metal scene was born.

As metalheads in bedrooms across the Middle East were getting tapes of bands from the US and Europe, others were discovering another style of music: hip hop. Originating in New York but later spreading to Los Angeles and then across the world, by the early 1990s the artists who would inspire young rappers in the Middle East were emerging: The Notorious B.I.G., Public Enemy, N.W.A. and, of course, Tupac.

In countries such as Lebanon, Egypt, Morocco and Tunisia, local rappers began writing in English and French and then switched to Arabic. For young Arabs in cities like Beirut, Tupac's lyrics about a tough life growing up in Los Angeles, as well as his family background in radical politics, resonated. Malikah, a Beiruti rapper who discovered Tupac in the late 1990s, described the American musician's significance: "I liked how he spoke his mind and he wasn't scared. He was rough yet still connected to his emotions. I felt like he was real in what he was doing. He had something to represent. He spoke about a lot more serious things than love and breakups that pop music talks about," she said.

It would be Tupac who would inspire Palestinian rapper Tamer Nafar to form DAM and ignite an explosion in the region's hip hop scene, the impact of which is still being felt today.

Musically, these two movements are very different but they share many similarities. Both were heavily influenced by western bands and artists and found their way to the Middle East via smuggled tapes and CDs and, later, satellite television. Once implanted in the Middle East, they gathered their own momentum and went their own way.

The change is more obvious in hip hop, simply because of the move from English to Arabic. The linguistic shift opened rap up to an indeterminable number of Arabic-speaking young people and popularised it amongst poorer Arabs in places including Syria, Egypt and Palestine.

By contrast, heavy metal was a middle-class movement in the Middle East. Its fans tended to be those who had friends who could travel abroad, but more significantly who spoke English and felt a cultural bond with America and Europe. The ferocity and irreverence of extreme metal appealed to young men and women cloistered in religiously conservative towns and cities. Like everywhere else in the world, it brought young people together in basements and bedrooms. It gave them something to do.

From the very beginning, extreme metal was frowned upon in the Middle East. Many of the people in this book have served time in jail, many have been beaten by police or soldiers and at least one has been flogged. Many are in exile, mostly because of state repression, but, in the case of Syrian musicians, because of war. Many are political, many are not, but most have been tarnished with the 'satanist' label at one time or another and have been punished accordingly.

Confess, an Iranian death metal band, were believed to be on bail at the time of my writing this book, but they faced many years in jail and the possibility of being sentenced to lashes after their arrest at the end of 2015. In Saudi Arabia, Iran and, at certain times, Egypt, Syria and Lebanon, rock and heavy metal music has been heavily curtailed – a situation that continues to this day. In fact, the only three states in the Middle East where metal and punk bands can perform and play (relatively) freely today are Israel, Lebanon and the UAE.

The are many reasons for this. First is the obvious association between rock, metal, hip hop and subversion – sex, drugs and rock 'n' roll. Malikah, as a woman, shocked many even in liberal Beirut when she stood up on stage and started rapping. Men who grew their hair long and began getting piercings and wearing black stood out on the streets of Cairo and Damascus. Some of the associations were fair: many fans were anti-religious, even if they didn't state it openly. Many used drugs, drank alcohol and opposed the state.

By definition they also looked to the West: their music and their style, whether hip hop or extreme metal, came from America and Europe. In a very few cases heavy metal has been Arabised: Saudi Arabia's al-Namrood use traditional Arab instruments, as do Melechesh, who were formed in Jerusalem. Egypt's Scarab draw heavily on Egyptian mythology in their lyrics. But the vast majority of bands in this book play forms of music – punk rock, death metal, doom – that were invented in the West.

At best, this has brought them ridicule and scorn from conservative elements of society that reject western liberalism and values. A Syrian metalhead told me that the authorities would coax cats into the police cells where metal fans were being held, and then watch to see if the young men would sacrifice them. An Egyptian recounted how he was frequently asked whether he had ever drunk blood.

At worst, heavy metal's 'otherness' has seen musicians cast as traitors or apostates. During the worst of the crackdowns on extreme metal in the Middle East, it was alleged that metal fans were agents of Israel because their headbanging imitated the praying of Orthodox Jews in Jerusalem. We may laugh at such ridiculous leaps of logic, except that in most of the countries included in this book, those allegations are deadly serious.

The second factor is that the rise of extreme metal and hip hop in the Middle East during the 1980s and 1990s came alongside a rise in radical Islamist movements, including Hezbollah and Hamas. It came as groups such as the Muslim Brotherhood grew in influence in Syria and in Egypt and just a few years after the Islamic revolution in Iran. It also came at a time when Saudi Arabia, flush with oil wealth, was spreading its hard-line strain of Wahhabi thought throughout the Middle East, and across the world.

This intolerant strain of Islam that started to dominate so much of the Middle East shared similarities with the fundamentalist strain of Christianity that picketed Kiss shows and tried to exploit the deaths of Raymond Belknap and James Vance in the witch-hunt against Judas Priest. If history has taught us anything, it is that extreme ideologies need enemies in order to survive. We will see in the following pages how alternative music, with all its associations, has proved a useful enemy – and how its supporters have paid a heavy price.

* * *

During the course of writing this book, I've asked a handful of questions what feels like a thousand times: When did you first get into metal? When did you first hear hip hop? What was your first punk rock record?

The answers have never disappointed me. A friend in Syria told me how he was nine years old and had just learned what would be a formative lesson about life in a police state (of which more later) when a friend handed him a pair of headphones and said: "Listen to this." It was Opeth, the Scandinavian band that remains immeasurably popular in the Middle East, and it made him feel better – it also changed his life. A Palestinian living in Yarmouk, the notorious refugee camp in Syria, had popped into a music store to pick up a Michael Jackson mix album for his uncle and the shop owner had asked him if he'd heard of this new rapper taking the US by storm: it was Eminem.

For some people, it was political: it was stories about Tupac's violent life that converted many young Arabs to hip hop, whether in Palestine, Lebanon or Egypt. But for some it wasn't: black metal fans in Iran weren't attracted to the lyrics of Norwegian bands because they were satanic, but rather because they told of freezing forests and mountains that reminded them of home.

At one point or another, all these people realised that they were not alone. In the days before the internet perhaps they saw another long-haired guy flicking through the heavy metal section in a backstreet record store, or another girl in a black T-shirt with a guitar slung over her shoulder. Maybe they struck up a conversation, maybe they started a band.

That is certainly how it began for me. I grew up in a small town where it was only natural that the few punks and metallers gravitated towards each other, shared music and eventually started bands. We persuaded pubs to host our gigs and played in front of crowds that usually consisted of our mates, the other bands, their girlfriends and a few bemused locals. When we visited London or Manchester for shows, we wrapped our demos in masking tape and tossed them onto the stage, in the hope that one of the bands would pick them up and call us and that we could achieve that hallowed realm: we could *make it*. At the time, reaching rock 'n' roll stardom was all we talked about, but on reflection it was about something much more important than that: we looked after each other and we believed in our music. We were a tribe.

I was aware that the tribe was bigger than us, but it was only after I moved to Shanghai in 2008, that I realised how big.

A mate and I had gone out to a local venue, Yuyintang, to watch a Scandinavian band that was passing through the city. We were standing in the crowd, holding pints of lager, our feet sticking to the beer-soaked floor, as three long-haired Chinese musicians – the support band – fiddled with amplifiers and mic stands on the stage. There was a sudden blast of noise and then they started playing some of the dirtiest death metal I have ever heard. It was so fast and loud and tight, the singer's vocals were so deep and brutal, and the drums blasted through the floor like a heartbeat. I was mesmerised.

After the show I went and found them as they were packing up and breathlessly tried to explain to them how incredible their set had been. The singer met my eyes for a second and then grabbed me in a bear hug. He was soaked with sweat and spoke no English but it didn't matter. He must have seen in my eyes that the music had connected. I tried for weeks to find out more about the band; all I managed was that they were from Anhui Province, a rural area a few hours from Shanghai. I still don't know their name.

It had never dawned on me that there was a grassroots metal scene in Asia but I immediately began seeking out bands wherever life as a journalist took me. In Malaysia, I found out about Sil Khannaz and the many other great punk and hardcore bands from that country. I became obsessed with the thriving punk rock scene in Chongqing, Beijing and, of course, Shanghai, where punk rock bands like Loudspeaker and experimental noise outfit Torturing Nurse played semi-regularly.

And then in 2010 I visited Saudi Arabia and met Ahmed, the lead singer of Saudi Arabian doom metal outfit Grieving Age. We had met just before prayer time so the entire city of Jeddah was shut down, every restaurant, every shop and cafe. We just drove up and down a dusty road talking about music, shouting over the din of industrial German metal. It didn't matter where or who we were. We were just two guys of a similar age talking about bands.

Ahmed put me in touch with someone, who connected me with someone else, and in the years since Jeddah I have spent many happy hours in the front seat of cars, on rooftops overlooking pulsing Arab cities, in dirty bars, in makeshift recording studios. I've been invited into people's homes and lives and treated like a brother simply because I knew the difference between Mayhem and Megadeth and could make a convincing case for preferring Guns N' Roses' *Use Your Illusion I* to *Use Your Illusion II*. In contrast to my regular life as a journalist, I haven't had to talk about politics or conflict or corruption. In some cases I have known someone for years without knowing whether they are Christian, Muslim or Druze. It just hasn't come up.

At times of violence, revolution and war, we've cranked up the stereo good and loud. We've let those fuzzy riffs and blast beats wash over us. We've ignored the outside world. We've drowned out the noise.

*   *   *

When the show was over in Abu Dhabi, Metallica stayed on stage for what felt like hours. James Hetfield grinned, his hands clasped together, bowing to the crowd. Lars Ulrich threw drumsticks, Kirk Hammett threw plectrums. Metallica, these four men we had idolised, with songs we knew as well as the streets we grew up on, seemed genuinely humbled.

As the crowd dispersed, we trudged across the arena, stumbling over discarded plastic pint glasses. Here and there, fans hovered, taking selfies, finishing beers, chatting in English and Arabic. I exchanged email addresses with a couple of Iranians who had flown in from Tehran. Over the next five years I would meet metalheads across the region who had been there and all of them said the same: that it had been special, that it had been important.

Because across the Arab world, heavy metal had always been there for them; young men and women had cranked up amps in basements and bedrooms. A few bands became internationally renowned, playing alongside some of the giants of the genre. Many, many more did not. They recorded a CD or two, played a couple of shows, and disbanded. But in *that* time and in *that* place they shut out the din of an ugly world. During the darkest of times, it was music that kept them going.

CHAPTER 1
LEBANON

It was a regular gig night at the Pavilion, al-Hamra, in as much as a gig night at the Pavilion was ever regular. Reverend Filthy Fuck was on top of the sound system, covered in his own blood, as guitarist Mullah Sadogoat broke beer bottles on his head. A few dozen other young men and women stood in haphazard groups in the main room of the venue, a former brothel, in a ramshackle district of Beirut. Filthy Fuck and Sadogoat made up the two-man black metal outfit Ayat and this was their first ever live gig, having been invited to join another of Beirut's extreme bands, Damaar, on stage.

It was 2006 and the war with Israel that would soon decimate the Lebanese capital was still a couple of months away. Not that violence was a stranger to any of the crowd: even those in their teens had been born in the dying days of Lebanon's 15-year civil war. Their parents had lived through those years of darkness when Hamra, Beirut's Sunni Muslim district, had been one of the world's most dangerous places, renowned for kidnappings, car bombs and firefights between rival militias.

Ayat's violent music had its origins in that world, just as the drug-fuelled debauchery of the Pavilion reflected a nihilism on the part of its bands. Clambering across speaker stacks as he screamed into a mic, it was fitting that Filthy Fuck had spilled blood on the beer-soaked stage of the Pavilion. Not so long ago the streets of Beirut had been awash with it.

Damaar had played their song 'Preaching for Mass Suicide' before inviting their mentors, Ayat – who were some years older – to perform 'Sacrifice' by Swedish black metal veterans Bathory. Together they played a number of songs from Ayat's album *Six Years of Dormant Hatred*, which is when Filthy Fuck cut his head on the ceiling and flew into a fury: "Some friends claimed that it was the most aggressive thing they have seen on stage in Beirut," recalled Safa, Damaar's guitarist, who that night was on a cocktail of booze, pills and opiates.

Every now and then word would go around that the cops were outside and the show would be raided, a daunting prospect not only given the open drug use by most of the crowd but because Lebanese police tended to frown on long-haired metalheads playing anti-religious music in underground venues. For Filthy Fuck, it was that fear that spurred him on. "We knew we would not be doing this again any time soon," he said. He was right: it would be the last time Ayat would perform in Lebanon.

It is not unusual for bands in the black metal genre to adopt pseudonyms, shun interviews and even refuse to ever play live, but for Filthy Fuck it was – and still is – practical. As one of very few openly anti-religious metal bands in the Middle East, Ayat's anonymity was a matter of life and death. The first track on their debut album, *All Hail Allah the Swine*, attracted controversy when it was released and continues to do so to this day. But Ayat are as contemptuous of Christianity – Lebanon's other main religion – as they are of Islam. Filthy Fuck mocks Christians with his adopted title 'Reverend' just as Sadogoat's 'Mullah' targets Muslim holy men.

Unlike other controversial bands across the region who sing in English, Ayat sing in Arabic, transporting their sacrilegious message far beyond the black metal scene. Expressed with a guttural scream that spews from the very pit of his stomach, Filthy Fuck's lyrics are not easy to make out, but their song titles have ensured that infamy has followed them. "We got a lot of publicity when we first came out as the first anti-Islamic band but we never perceived ourselves as such. We dealt with organised religion as a whole," Filthy Fuck said.

The Pavilion was called a lot of things, including 'The Whorehouse' in tribute to its former life, but Filthy Fuck summed it up in one word: horrid. The building had ceased functioning as a brothel in the 1980s, as the civil war raged, and had been left empty until it was taken over by the dozen or so Hamra bands in early 2004. Owned by a sympathetic local businessman known as 'The Spider', the venue was a narrow corridor of 5 by 25 metres with a bar close to the entrance. In the back were three smaller rooms that were turned into jamming spaces for local bands. The venue was opened every two weeks by the bands to host metal shows, and the rest of the time was just a place to hang out, smoke weed or drop acid and play.

At the Pavilion, Filthy Fuck remembered, anything went: "It was truly abject – in a good way. You'd have rooms and passageways, and in one you'd have a death metal guitarist, a punk drummer and some thrash vocalist jamming, people listening; in the other room a couple would be fucking; at the bar people would be downing shots and laughing."

The bands were a mish-mash of genres, from old school punk to death and black metal, but they were united by both a love of extreme music and an outright contempt for outsiders. "The Pavilion witnessed the birth of another kind of metal scene," said Safa, the Damaar guitarist, who started hanging out at the Pavilion in his early teens. "It didn't revolve around metal, but attitude."

For Filthy Fuck, the rebellious spirit that would find itself channelled into the violent music of Ayat had its origins in growing up in Lebanon, for better and for worse. He remembers how, as a kid in a Shia Muslim area of Beirut that was rapidly being taken over by the political movement Hezbollah, his father would deliberately flout the Ramadan fast by having lavish barbecues on his balcony, baiting his pious neighbours with the smell of freshly cooked meat. He recalled:

> He was a very strict man, joyless and angry, a little bit like I am today, but he knew his principles well and did not appreciate it when people encroached on his rights. So when the talk in town was that eating in public was becoming increasingly frowned upon, Dad was doing his barbecues on the balcony, wearing a white wife-beater, fanning the coals in his boxer shorts. The whole neighbourhood would be on their balconies staring at us, and Dad would be staring back at them with a deathly stare that could melt an iceberg. It was incredible. And I could not keep my mouth shut since then.

Getting into metal meant being part of a very small club in Beirut, and Filthy Fuck remembered that seeing another metalhead on the streets wearing a Bathory T-shirt was a big deal. But he found early on that Ayat's abrasive, anti-religious style did not fit well with the mainstream scene in Lebanon. The animosity peaked with the release of Ayat's first EP, which branded the Prophet Mohammed a murderer and a rapist. Soon after, mainstream metallers in Beirut began to openly snub Ayat and the other Hamra bands.

Since the late 1990s, the Beirut metal scene outside Hamra had been mainly centred around the eastern Christian districts of Ashrafieh and Gemmayzeh, and promoters even brought international acts to Lebanon, despite regular problems with the police and the church. For years, metalheads had battled accusations that they were satanists or subversives – now Ayat waltzed onto the scene and performed music that seemed to confirm everything that the authorities had been saying. "It was like an earthquake," Filthy Fuck said. "I'm sure it felt to them that we had undermined all their efforts of respectability by providing the anti-metal brigade with all the ammunition they needed." But he was unrepentant. As far as he was concerned, heavy metal should attack the authorities, be they religious or political, and the efforts of the mainstream metal scene to attract sponsors and bring international acts to Lebanon made them sell-outs.

Open hatred of religion in heavy metal is as old as the genre itself, but while it has been an integral part of extreme music in Europe and the US, it is rare in the Middle East. Even in countries like Iran, which have established black metal scenes, bands generally avoid attacking Islam (for obvious reasons, given that blasphemy in the Islamic Republic is punishable by death). Egypt's horrendous crackdown of the

1990s, which saw metallers dragged from the streets, jailed and persecuted for their black clothes and long hair, was directly provoked by a crowd member raising an inverted cross at a live show. Perhaps as a result, the overwhelming majority of Middle East metal fans and musicians condemn the few satanic or anti-religious metal bands that exist in the region, first among them Ayat.

The band did, however, have its acolytes. Safa was a teenage death metal fan when he first heard Ayat, but within months he had formed Damaar and made the shift to openly anti-religious black metal. From the outset, Damaar and their fans had problems with the authorities: "We were bullied by the police most of the time as we sat on the street because of the way we looked. Most of my friends had harsh encounters with authorities because of metal and devil worship," he said.

As a result, the mainstream metal scene began to cut them loose. When band members tried to attend shows elsewhere in Beirut, they would find their names on a blacklist at the door. Even when they did get in, they would often be turfed out by security guards for moshing – the rough-and-tumble that takes place in the front few rows of a heavy metal show was banned at most legitimate venues in the city. But this treatment only reinforced the siege mentality among the bands. It created a tight-knit, insular scene that decades later would still be remembered as a high-water mark for Middle East metal.

Like its metal scene, Hamra was for decades cut off from the east of Beirut as rival militias fought for control of the city, and even today its character is unique. A Muslim district, Hamra is also home to the American University of Beirut and, even during the war, the bulk of international embassies and missions. It was – and remains – a liberal neighbourhood where mosques sit alongside cafes and bars and university students mix with retirees and office workers.

This liberalism made it an obvious hub for the alternative music scene, from hip hop to heavy metal and punk rock. Long before Palestinian hip hop became a global phenomenon, Beiruti rappers were meeting in abandoned bomb shelters and parking lots and writing songs. Eslam Jawaad, a Lebanese-Syrian rapper, remembers there being a tiny hip hop scene as far back as 1994. "We're talking on the street level. There were no venues. It was bunkers or buildings or somebody's front room," he said. Lynn Fattouh, another Lebanese rapper known as Malikah, said that even when she started out at the end of 2000 there was very little tolerance for alternative genres such as hip hop: "They thought that we were trying to act like Americans, that we were fake. They made fun of how we dressed."

While Beirut's rappers confined themselves to parking lots and the occasional house party, the punk and metal scene converged on 'the Alley', a small lane just off Hamra's main drag where, from 2001, punks and metallers would hang out, trade cassettes and CDs and form bands. Just as the adversity that faced the hip hop scene forced Lebanese rappers to form lasting bonds (Malikah and Eslam perform together to this day), so the Alley created partnerships that would define the Hamra scene for years to come. "A great band from Lebanon had to come from Hamra," said Tex, the founder of thrash outfit Nightchains and punk rock band Detox. "We set a standard and you had to meet that. You didn't have to live in Hamra, but you had to be here," he said.

Even in their teens, Tex and his ex-wife Aida were heavily influenced by the UK punk scene and remember trading tapes of seminal bands such as Crass, whose anarchic and raw music resonated so fully with Lebanon's punks. Their access to these bands came via Aida, who regularly travelled overseas with her parents and brought back music that would never have been available in Lebanon. Tex started his first band in 2004 and soon the group moved into the Pavilion, refitting the sprawling warren of rooms into a bar and practice space for bands.

Much of the reason for Pavilion was necessity: Tex's bands could not get away with playing anywhere else. But while Filthy Fuck remembers being shunned openly by the mainstream metal scene in the east, Tex plays down any rivalry, especially any suggestion that the division was on religious grounds – given that the east of Beirut is mostly Christian and the west Muslim. He is clearly sensitive about journalists using sectarianism to explain either his music or his country. For Tex, the difference between the Hamra scene and the rest of Beirut was simply one of musical style and ethics:

> It wasn't about competition, it was two different scenes. If they were Iron Maiden then we were Venom. They liked their sound clean and we liked it dirty. We just got too excited sometimes. We were self-righteous. We thought what we were doing was the best. We had a lot of fights and we were violent. We knew we were better.

It was natural that Ayat and Damaar fitted into Tex's aspiration for the Hamra scene. He had played with Damaar's members Nadim and Nabil in Nightchains and persuaded the band to record an EP, *Triumph*, which they released in 2005.

Ayat also found a home at the Pavilion. Although musically their extreme black metal was far removed from the punk rock and thrash of many of the Pavilion bands, Ayat's anti-religious stance excited Hamra veterans such as Tex. "They thought our records were bibles, they acted like we did and rejected the same things," Filthy Fuck said. "It was a delightful surprise when we saw that there was a whole offshoot of the metal scene who actually saw us as proper innovators and an inspiration, rather than the pest status we had to endure everywhere else."

But while he believes that Ayat played a role in the foundation of one of the Middle East's most notorious scenes, he attributes all the real work to Tex, Aida and the early Hamra punks. "I like to believe we played a part in the creation of this little movement by providing a starting point and a few records unlike anything else created at that time. But the actual work on the ground? They did everything and we just popped in every now and then to cheers and free drinks. That's the extent of our actual physical contribution," he said.

It was not so unusual that two vastly different styles of music would find a joint cause amidst the disorder of 2000s Lebanon. Black metal as a genre owed much of its anarchic spirit and DIY ethic to the 1970s British punk scene. It was an English band, Venom, who gave a name to a style of music that would later be refined by Bathory and later Norwegian bands Mayhem, Emperor and Burzum. Venom were influenced heavily by Black Sabbath and Motörhead, both British bands. Both Venom and Bathory – considered the two most important bands in the first wave of black metal – leaned heavily on the fast riffs and two-beat groove of punk rock. Bathory's 1984 self-titled album has more in common with UK punk bands like Discharge and GBH than it does with the genre that is today known as black metal.

The similarities are more than stylistic: the satanism that has always been so integral to black metal was, at least for early bands, a rebellious philosophy rather than a religious one. While many musicians – first among them Denmark's Mercyful Fate – would later adopt the satanic religion then popularised by Anton LaVey, the decision of Black Sabbath to place an inverted cross on the back sleeve of their 1970 debut album was intended as a 'fuck you' to Christian sensibilities rather than an affirmation of Luciferian faith. Even LaVey described his satanism as an *inversion* of Christianity rather than a religion itself: it was about embracing those things – sex, drugs, freedom and sin – that Christianity forbade, rather than replacing one faith with another.

In Britain and later in the US, this would create issues for heavy metal across genres. But in Lebanon, the existence of anti-religious bands such as Ayat and Damaar was more than inflammatory. It was dangerous.

The Pavilion's time as the central hub of Hamra's punk and metal scene was short, from 2004 to the summer of 2006, when war broke out between Hezbollah and Israel and bombs rained down on the Lebanese capital. Many of Hamra's punks and metalheads left the country during the war and most did not return. Tex moved to Denmark with Aida and worked as a roadie, carrying amplifiers for a stage management company. He hated Denmark and for one year he recorded no music. By the time he returned to Beirut in 2007, people had started changing. "When we were young, before the war, we all used to drink, but after the war people started doing drugs. We used to really love the music, but when the drugs came in it changed," he said.

Filthy Fuck also noted the effect that drugs had on the Hamra scene. The drug of choice was weed, but many of the crowd dabbled in harder substances too – such as LSD and opium. He regrets all these years later that younger and more vulnerable members of the scene followed his example. "I was struggling with addiction but as one of the senior members of that scene, I heard it more often than I would like that many had started drugs to emulate me. In my later years that was something that bothered me very much," he said.

As for the Pavilion, the building was demolished soon after the war and is now a car park, providing a few dozen parking spaces to Beirutis for a couple of pounds an hour. It was an ignoble end to something that once defined a generation.

For Filthy Fuck, it was the end of an era. He said:

The Whorehouse was the epitome and the swansong all at once. We had this massive explosion of creativity where we had a scene for the first time. A place where all the misfits gathered, bands were created, collaborations were made left and right between the most surprising people. But the end was almost definitive. All the bands from that time broke up, the location was lost, most figureheads of that period went into seclusion, us included, and things died down.

* * *

It is no surprise that the term 'like Beirut' entered the lexicon of our modern age as meaning something chaotic, disorderly or violent. For 15 years, the Lebanese capital was racked with destruction and death, and although the conflict ended in 1990, the stigma has remained. Ask most people in the West what figure they associate with Beirut and they are unlikely to say Fairuz, the legendary singer and first 'diva' of the Middle East, but rather Terry Waite, the British hostage who spent five years chained to a radiator as a prisoner of militant group Hezbollah.

But Beirut wasn't always a byword for violence and destruction. For decades after its independence from France, the city was a safe haven for writers, musicians and dissidents from elsewhere in the Arab world. It became a hub for music, literature and journalism, attracting not just Arab exiles but foreign explorers, diplomats, writers and spies. It was home to Christians, Druze, Shia and Sunni Muslims. Often fluent in English, French and Arabic, Beirutis drew from the Middle East and Europe in equal measure. As Samir

Kassir writes in his moving portrait of the city, 'Beirut', it was "a veritable paradise. An Arab city that was nonetheless foreign: a foreign city that was nonetheless Arab."

But in the mid-1970s, Beirut descended into an orgy of sectarian violence that saw the city split down the middle, with Muslims on one side and Christians on the other. Lebanon's neighbours waded into the conflict, which at one point involved nationals of some 38 countries, from Nepali peacekeepers to Israeli soldiers, Iraqi mercenaries to Palestinian militants.

By the middle of the 1980s, Israel occupied much of the south of the country and Syria controlled the rest, as Lebanese and Palestinian militants butchered each other in the streets. The foreigners who had once flocked to Beirut fled in the face of kidnappings and murders. The perception of Beirut as a freewheeling and quasi-European gateway to the Orient was replaced by a starker image: that of the bombed-out US embassy building after a suicide attack that killed 63 marines in 1983.

Lydia Canaan grew up in this Beirut. As a child, her father had taken her to Hamra and she still recalls the colours and smells of the markets. Like many Christians, she lived in one of the towns that dots Mount Lebanon, Brummana, miles from the violence of the front line, but the conflict was a constant presence. On their radios, residents would hear reports of shelling, sniper fire and atrocities. She first heard of many of the Muslim districts of west Beirut – Hamra and Ouzai – as well as cities like Nabatieh in the context of terrorist attacks or rocket fire. Even up high on Mount Lebanon, friends and family became victims of the fighting. "War caused me to grow up faster. I learned to never take anything or anyone for granted," she said. "It taught me to treasure loved ones, because they could be lost in the blink of an eye."

As a conflict raged, Lydia felt that heavy metal music just seemed to make sense. She had grown up listening to music in the three languages she spoke – French, English and Arabic – but had always been drawn to western bands such as Abba and the Bee Gees. She soon migrated to heavier bands such as Journey, Iron Maiden and Ronnie James Dio, and in 1983 she responded to an advert in a newspaper from a local group, Equation, who were looking for a lead singer.

When she arrived at the audition the band told her they were actually looking for a man, but they were so impressed with her voice that they took her on anyway. Equation practised for nine months before their first show at the Chateau Trianon theatre, in east Beirut. Driving out of the hills, Lydia recalled hitting a huge traffic jam on the way into the city and had to get out of the car and walk the final few miles to the venue. It was only then that she realised that the packed cars, buses and vans were heading for Chateau Trianon.

Soon after the show, Lydia began writing her own material. "Heavy metal was the way I needed to talk about being against the war and against violence," she said. "It gave me a lot of adrenaline, to speak out." She followed her show with others and Equation became famous for arranging concerts amidst the flare-ups of violence, and even under rocket fire. In the midst of all the bloodshed, the sight of a teenager decked out in leather and singing heavy metal songs in front of thousands of people brought everyone from schoolchildren to militia fighters to Equation's shows, despite the risks. It was part of the fatalism that began to take root in the minds of many Lebanese as the war lengthened from months to years. "We didn't even know if we were going to make it or not. If we made a date to perform, we didn't know if anyone was going to show up," she said.

It wasn't only fellow Christians who would attend her shows. Often when she was on stage, fans would push to the front of the crowd and shout up at her. They would tell her that they had come from Muslim districts of Hamra and Ouzai, from Tripoli and Baalbek, from the southern cities of Sidon and Tyre, then under Israeli occupation. They had crossed the front lines to attend her shows, risking kidnap and death, snipers and car bombs. "They would say all of these names of cities and villages and places that I had either never heard of, or that I associated with terrorism and war," she said. In a country that in 1985 was the antithesis of co-existence, its capital divided along sectarian lines, heavy metal had done what guns, bombs and diplomacy had failed to do: it had brought Lebanese people together. "I was so proud as an artist, and as a Christian," she said.

But such examples of co-existence were rare in a city bitterly divided along religious lines. Lebanon may have been designed as a pluralist state but Christian, Muslim and Druze factions were backed by powerful strongmen and their militias, as well as foreign interests. Syria backed Hezbollah, Israel the Christians, Iraq the Palestinians. At the end of the conflict, much of the country was in ruins.

Like many other Lebanese, Lydia had left in the late 1980s, in her case for Switzerland, determined to make something of her life in Europe as her country imploded. When the Lebanese war finally ended, she returned to Beirut and immediately headed downtown, an area she had not visited since she was a child. She stood in Martyrs' Square, the former front line, where Italian sculptor Renato Marino Mazzacurati's iconic statue of Lebanese freedom fighters executed during the Ottoman era sat on its pedestal, riddled with bullet holes. She remembered downtown Beirut as a colourful, vibrant place, far removed from the carnage that 15 years of fighting had wreaked on the ancient city. Martyrs' Square was once Beirut's bus and taxi terminus (as well as its red light district) but, as she looked around, Lydia reflected that beneath the rubble at her feet probably lay thousands of corpses. "I stood there among the ruins and I burst into tears. I thought how if you just excavated through the rubble, how many bodies would you find? And for what?" she said. "For what?"

The downtown district of Beirut where Lydia had stood that day was rebuilt, but the city's scars remained. Almost a quarter of a million Lebanese had fled during the conflict and those who remained still wrestled with what had happened. The war was over, but it lived on. "It was an interesting time in Beirut in the mid-1990s. It was a couple of years after the war ended but the tension was still there," said Eslam Jawaad, the rapper, who had been living in the US but returned after the conflict.

Israel occupied the south of Lebanon until 2000 and flare-ups between rival militias were common. Hezbollah, the only Lebanese militia that continued to operate after the agreement that ended the war, grew in influence. Lebanon was never really *not* at war, even during peacetime. "Throughout my years there, Israel bombed a number of times. You've always been a part of some form of war, it hasn't really stopped," said Jawaad.

But the end of the conflict also saw the emergence of new venues in the city, where rappers in particular could perform. Gemmayzeh, the Christian district to the east of Martyrs' Square, began to develop. And then, in 1997, Ziad Hamdan and Yasmine Hamdan founded one of Lebanon's most important bands, Soap Kills. Their name was a criticism of the fact that in the six years since the guns fell silent and Beirut was reunified, Beirutis had still not found a way to deal with what had happened. With the brand-new buildings that post-war Prime Minister Rafik Hariri was having built downtown, they had tried to wash themselves clean. But it was killing them.

Ziad grew up in the worst days of the Lebanese civil war and the streets around his home still bear the pockmarks of shells and small arms fire. But as the war raged around him, his parents did everything they could to make sure he wasn't witness to the violence.

> My parents were very open. They never said no to anything. I grew up in a bubble. I was in a warzone but in my house was a love zone. So I didn't feel the war – I heard it and I saw it. In my house there was tolerance and love and no fear. It gave me strength and courage.

Ziad met Yasmine at secondary school. "I fell in love," he said. Before the pair began making music together, Ziad would have Yasmine model for him and would develop pictures of her. He knew that Yasmine wanted to be a singer, so he promised that together they would form a band. "I didn't have a project of doing music in my life – I was just in love with Yasmine and I had to have her forever. Her dream was to do music so I said, yeah let's do music," he said.

Ziad bought a Roland 303 drum machine but had little idea how to use it. He began playing basic rhythms as Yasmine sang traditional Arabic music over the top. Even years later that simplicity has been retained. Ziad is still amused when fans ask how they came up with it and he has to respond that it was just a lack of experience. Their songs would typically imitate the style of traditional Arabic music but fuse the melodies over drum and bass or dub. Their lyrics are about love, not just romantic love but love for the city, its sounds and its scars.

It was the scars that fascinated a young Ziad. As he reached his late teens, Hariri had come to power and Beirut became a construction site. New developments were designed in the style of the old but they were cleaner, more organised. They imitated the architectural style of post-war Beirut but they were new – for Ziad, it was an attempt by the older generation who had lived through the conflict to put it behind them without accepting what had happened. He said:

Soap Kills referred to how there was a big clean-up of the city without a reflection on the reasons of the war. Why did communities end up butchering each other? This cannot be solved with just a clean-up of the town. A generation does not have any references. And even the war is erased. They don't know who they are and why they have gone through what they've gone through.

Ziad saw it as unhealthy to put such destruction and death in the past: Lebanon must cleanse itself of what took place. "It isn't wrong to ask questions. It doesn't mean we are not moving on. Asking your parents how they ended up carrying a gun and shooting at their neighbours? How does asking that keep you from moving on?" he said.

For the Lebanese, Soap Kills came at the right time: "Yasmine was such a beauty and I had this twist of dirt – it was like beauty and beast, you know. And our lyrics were honest. It is not deep poetry but it was really honest," he said. Unlike many bands that aped western music and sang in English, Soap Kills were able to attract as many fans of Arabic music as Beirutis who were listening to British rock or American jazz. "We had everything to be adopted by the Arab crowd. We had everything that would make an Arab proud. Arabic classical music is so huge but for modern Arabic music there is very little references. We made them proud to say: this is the new Arabic music. In that sense we were important."

In one song, 'Aranis', Yasmine sings about a trip to the coast with her lover over the sound of a plucked guitar. She mimics the sound of the street vendors selling corn – *aranis* in Arabic. After the first verse, the song changes tempo and shifts into reggae: the subject changes, describing the colonial era, when French expatriates would dress in fine clothes and give the impression of respectability but at night frequent brothels and smoke opium. Yasmine's voice goes from soft to harsh and mocking, the Arabic rasped rather than sung. These two worlds both had open and hidden realms. For the colonial French, it was public and private life; for the lovers, it was their private discourse as opposed to the street scene around them. For Lebanon too, there was what was visible and what was hidden.

Other songs were more direct, and it was one of these that finally got Soap Kills banned from the radio and destroyed both the band and Ziad and Yasmin's relationship. "The lyrics were very simple: 'Why are you angry? What are you afraid of? What are you hiding from? You're not a man, you're not a man,'" Ziad said. The issue wasn't just that the song was political, but that it questioned the social mores of Lebanon by having a woman effectively taunting a man about his masculinity. The band shot a video and approached a TV channel to play it, but the channel refused, arguing that their Saudi financial backers would not tolerate a song that had a woman addressing a man in such a way.

It was the beginning of the end for Soap Kills. Word got around and radio stations began to refuse to play any of their material: the duo was effectively locked out. For Yasmine, it was a permanent barrier to her career as a singer and she knew that she had to leave Lebanon to follow her dreams. "Yasmine wanted to pursue a career abroad because she realised that she could never evolve here. It killed the band," he said.

* * *

Soap Kills were of the generation that was born during the war but did not fight in it. But as they created new forms of Arabic popular music, others looked to rock and heavy metal.

Bassem Deaibess, the frontman of Lebanese metal band Blaakyum, one of the country's best-known groups, grew up in Qatar and spent his early teenage years as an obsessive Michael Jackson fan. When he returned to Lebanon, he attended a Christian school and used to entertain the other students by recording pop songs and dancing.

He was given a mix tape by a cousin that included both Scorpions and Body Count, the American heavy metal band fronted by rapper Ice-T. Bassem soon discovered Guns N' Roses, buying *Use Your Illusion I* and *II*, and persuaded his father to buy him a guitar, a $400 Les Paul copy that looked like the one played by Slash. Disappointed that it didn't sound distorted as on the albums of Iron Maiden and Metallica, he would crank the volume up louder and louder until he got a similar effect.

Bassem formed Blaakyum in 1995 and the band performed the first heavy metal show in Lebanon since the end of the war. Then, in May of that year, a Lebanese teenager shot himself in his bedroom surrounded by posters of Nirvana and Kurt Cobain, who had killed himself a year earlier, and left a suicide note asking that all his CDs be buried with him. A Christian TV channel picked up the story, claiming that heavy metal and rock music were encouraging young people to commit suicide: "His father went on TV and said that he died because of hard rock," Bassem said.

The incident came just four years after British heavy metal band Judas Priest had stood trial over the deaths of two fans, who claimed that subliminal messages in the song 'Better By You, Better Than Me' urged them to shoot themselves. The band had been acquitted but the allegations of subliminal messages in heavy metal persisted. In Lebanon, the death of the young Nirvana fan came alongside allegations that heavy metal was linked to Zionism and Israel, with the media making the tenuous link that headbanging looked like Jews praying at the Western Wall.

By 1996, the government was arresting young people and dragging them into police stations, while the Interior Ministry published a blacklist that listed Nirvana and a number of other bands. One rock venue where Blaakyum were playing was raided and Bassem and his bandmates only escaped by hiding behind the bar. The organisers were arrested, bundled into police cars and taken to prison.

In 1998, Bassem was arrested for the first time. "I was at a military checkpoint and I was taken by the military police – and that's when I went to jail. They saw the way I was dressed and my long black hair. They said: Do you like Nirvana? Do you like Metallica? And then they drove me to prison." Bassem was asked at length about the many lurid allegations that had appeared in the media since the heavy metal crackdown began. He was asked whether he went to communion, because one story had alleged that heavy metal fans used to take the Catholic ritual and keep the wafers that are distributed so that they could later desecrate them. Ironically, Bassem was still a committed Christian in the 1990s; he didn't become an atheist until later.

He was also asked how he felt about cats, due to the rumour that metal fans sacrificed animals at their shows. "Three of my friends were arrested at another time and the guards let three cats loose in the cell, just to see what they would do," Bassem recalled. "In the end they just gave up. They said: 'You must not be in the Nirvana sect,' and they let me go."

The furore died down and bands were able to play again, but a few years later the authorities once again turned their attention to Beirut's metal community. "It was much worse than in 1996. It was so bad that we could not walk in the streets with long hair and wear black T-shirts." Bassem had his guitar confiscated in a police raid. He had been using the basement of a church as a practice space but after a neighbour told the pastor that the bands were using it to perform black masses, they had to move.

The bands kept a low profile but their reputation even spread to neighbouring Syria, where there was a well-established scene centred around Aleppo, Homs and Damascus. Once when Bassem was due to perform in Aleppo, the gig was raided by the police. The authorities said that they were looking for a Lebanese satanist believed to be in Syria converting young Syrians to the dark arts – as one of only a few Lebanese musicians at the show, it was pretty clear that they believed it to be Bassem. Luckily, he had been tipped off and quickly ran to the venue's toilets, where he shaved off his beard and donned a bright red T-shirt. He then headed out to a nearby recording studio owned by a friend and waited for two hours before it was safe for him to flee Syria and head back to Beirut.

In 2005, the assassination of Rafik Hariri and the street protests that followed ended 30 years of Syrian occupation. It led to a new era in Lebanon, banishing Syria's feared secret police – the *Mukhabarat* – and giving Beirut's metallers a new lease of life. Many of those in the scene were involved in the protests, during which a broad section of Lebanese society called for 'Freedom, Sovereignty and Independence'.

Even those who objected to Hariri were outraged that a man who stood up to Bashar al-Assad could be executed in the middle of a Beirut street by terrorists acting with impunity. Hezbollah, Assad's proxy, was blamed for the attack, and, after the protests swelled, Syria withdrew its forces from Lebanon.

Bassem opened a bar and live music venue, Cherries, which became a hub for the local metal scene and a regular venue for shows. Over in Hamra, Filthy Fuck, Tex and Damaar had moved into the Pavilion. Yasmine, from Soap Kills, had gone solo, leaving Ziad to form a new band, The New Government. He released a self-titled track blaming the country's elites for the recent spate of assassinations that had culminated in the murder of Hariri. "I killed the prime minister / I killed the famous journalist / We're the new government, we're the new government," it said.

And then came the war with Israel. Over three weeks, Israel pounded Beirut and southern Lebanon with airstrikes in response to Hezbollah rockets fired from the south. Before he left Beirut, Tex and some of the Hamra crowd used to gather in a bar close to the Pavilion and watch the explosions as Israeli bombs rained down on the predominantly Shia suburbs in the south of the city. On the other side of Beirut Bassem and the other members of Blaakyum would hole up in bomb shelters and write songs.

The conflict was ugly and brutal and for many it brought back memories of the dark days of the civil war. For some musicians, it made their message more radical – more political. Malikah, the rapper, had moved to Canada but remembers that it was the 2006 war with Israel that led to her abandoning English lyrics in favour of Arabic. "That war in particular was a key year in my life. Everything changed for me. In the very beginning my music wasn't political. It was about my life, about random shit, but in 2006 when the war happened, yeah it became more political," she said. It was a hard lesson, seeing her country bombarded on television from thousands of miles away, but it was a pivotal one, and in many ways it made her the rapper she is today.

Yasmine left Lebanon for Paris, and Ziad fell in and out of bands before forming Ziad and the Wings. They recorded a reggae track, 'General Suleiman', about a Lebanese general, Michel Suleiman, who was running for president. The song acknowledged Suleiman's military record but called for him, his militiamen and the army in general to "go home". The band performed it regularly and recorded a video, which was posted online.

Ziad was arrested for defamation. His arrest coincided with the Arab Spring and was picked up by news organisations across the world after Ziad instructed his lawyer to post a statement of protest on Facebook. Eventually, the government buckled and released him.

For many musicians, his treatment reflected the fact that, although the Syrian occupation was over, Beirut was not free. Even today, bands have to submit their lyrics to the Interior Ministry before gigs and, because those working at the ministry rarely speak English, they have to be translated into Arabic. Lebanon still has an official blacklist of albums that cannot be brought into the country.

Lydia Canaan blames the Syrian occupation of Lebanon, which only ended in 2005, and the entrenchment of the authoritarian Syrian Baathist state. With Syria's feared secret police stalking the streets and looking for outward signs of dissent, particularly amongst the Lebanese youth, the entire art scene had little choice but to comply.

Lydia had been branded the first rock star of the Middle East as her profile rose throughout the 1990s and early 2000s. But while Arabic pop music is dominated by female stars, the rock and heavy metal world in both Lebanon and the Middle East more widely has never witnessed a tipping of the scales towards female performers. "I was hoping that other girls would go on stage and perform heavy metal – that I would open a door, a pathway. But I am so disappointed that there isn't anybody today – no female going on stage and singing hard rock," she said. "It's cool that I am the first rock star of the Middle East but I would like to see so many more women, because I am a feminist."

Malikah has been referred to as the Queen of Middle East hip hop since she first attracted attention on the scene by winning a competition on Lebanese TV, but, again, she has been joined by only a handful of female rappers throughout the Middle East. "Now I would say we are five, even less – not as much as you would hope there would be," she said.

Sadly, in the ten years since Syrian military rule ended in Lebanon, the heavy metal witch-hunt has returned regularly. In 2012 a shock-jock journalist known as Joe Malouf began running sensational news programmes about heavy metal fans holding satanic masses and sacrificing cats. This time, Bassem didn't take it lying down: "I called in. I said: 'Listen, we thought these days were behind us.'"

After he spoke on the show he was detained again, this time for 12 hours, but he noticed a change in the way in which the police dealt with him. "He kept asking if I was a good Christian and I would say I was born a Christian but I don't believe. And then he'd say to the supervisor, 'You see, he is a good Christian.'" But increasingly it is not the authorities damning Lebanon's metal scene, but practicalities: there are not enough venues, and those there are don't want to put on heavy metal shows. "It is getting harder and harder to put on metal events now," he said, "either you lose money or you just break even." Not that money matters to him, he is quick to add: "It is not like we don't want our music to be famous – we do – but we play music because it is our culture. It isn't a choice."

As for the authorities, Bassem still gets riled at the media scare stories and frequently appears on TV or on the radio, defending the scene. But like many Lebanese musicians, he actually felt freer during the war. "In the civil war – and in the 2006 war – you didn't give it a second thought. You were in the shelter and you had a guitar and the radio and nothing else to do – nobody questioned you." It is an observation that Lydia Canaan echoes. For all the death and destruction of the conflict, the war gave Lydia freedom. "The crazy thing is that I felt more free as an artist and as an individual to express myself during the war – much more than I am today. How insane must that sound?"

* * *

As far as the Beirut scene now is concerned, the younger generation is equally despondent. New bands occasionally form but, as is often the case with heavy metal, they have thrived in the most unlikely of places. One such example is the northern city of Tripoli, where the headlines during the Syrian civil war have mostly been about gun battles and Sunni militants.

One band, Hatecrowned, have released two albums of furious black metal right out of the Ayat and Damaar playbook. Ayvaal, 22, founded the band in 2011, during the worst of the street fighting in Tripoli between Sunni and Alawite militias: "Mortars would fall in our neighbourhood like random raindrops, shops and streets would shut down,

Salafists were spread like stray cats everywhere in the city. There were assassinations, car bombs in busy parts of the city – that kind of stuff."

Ayvaal said that, contrary to the belief of those inside and outside Lebanon that Tripoli is a city filled with Islamists, at least a dozen bands from both the black and death metal genres have recorded and released albums in the last few years – even if most of them have since split. Unlike older metallers, Ayvaal had the benefit of social media and the internet to connect him to bands such as Burzum and Death, whereas his predecessors had to rely on the radio or on tapes brought into the country. As a result of this, perhaps, Hatecrowned's music – as complex as it is impeccably recorded – shows a maturity far beyond their years.

But just as Filthy Fuck found himself banned from gigs in Beirut due to Ayat's irreligious message, so Ayvaal also found Hatecrowned excluded. Luckily, he feels that black metal should never seek to be accepted. "They cannot swallow the fact that Hatecrowned was a straightly satanic band and they think that black metal is just noise," he said.

He recalled hearing Ayat for the first time when he was 16 and being impressed as much by the lyrics as by the music. Even though he was too young to have attended gigs at the Pavilion or hung out in the Alley in the early years, he speaks of that time as a golden age. "Musicians back then played metal for the sake of it and for the passion they had for this music. Not anymore – they cannot make a living out of it and no one is born rich here," he said.

Despite the open antipathy to religion in Hatecrowned's lyrics, Ayvaal has not had run-ins with pious Muslims in Tripoli, despite his multiple tattoos and piercings, his black T-shirt and beard: "All they do is look at me and I look back at them and it ends up with both sides staring at each other. With all the power they have, they never have the will for a close fight."

The veterans agree that the scene is not what it was. Ziad and Yasmine recently sold their back catalogue to an international label and Soap Kills have achieved a fame 20 years after their inception that they never had in the short time they were a band. But for Ziad this fame has proved a double-edged sword. He often finds that producers in the city won't work with him. "If I go to a producer he will say: 'But you are a legend, you don't need me!' I am condemned to this underground world. It has been over 20 years and I am still small, you know," he said. "Soap Kills is a beautiful thing that happened to me and my biggest pride – but it is also like a curse."

Since his arrest, Ziad has focused mainly on producing and has become disenchanted with Lebanese rock:

I feel the scene is so clean – clean kids that you could introduce your parents to. And even though the country is so corrupt and there are so many things to be told. There are heroes needed and nobody is stepping up. Even the guys who pierce their noses and tongues and tattoo themselves – they don't confront the situation.

Ziad has spent the last two years producing other musicians, as well as attending shows in his search for the heroes who will use their music to turn against the 'banana republic' that he considers the Lebanese state to be. It is not just about politics, he said, but a search for music that will affect him in the same way that he was once moved by Yasmine and Soap Kills – in the same way that he feels when he hears David Bowie.

He has recently begun producing an Egyptian singer called Maryam Saleh, a rising star who performs modern versions of the political songs of Sheikh Imam, the late Egyptian musician who was an icon of the revolutionary student movement. In her unique music, he sees similarities with the music of Soap Kills and of Yasmine:

I always search. I always hope that someone can shake me, move me. I just hope to be moved every time I go to watch a show. This is the pleasure I get in my life – meeting inspiring people and sharing in that inspiration This is more important than

the exposure and the fame – just waking up and
being excited.

* * *

Late in the summer of 2016, Tex marked the ten-year
anniversary of the infamous Ayat and Damaar gig at the
Pavilion. After the show someone had taken a picture of the
Hamra crowd, which had been printed on the inside jacket
of a Nightchains CD, alongside a handful of other shots
of gigs and good times at the venue. Damaar were there,
and so were Ayat. Filthy Fuck stood alongside four or five
other metalheads; Safa played guitar in another. A punk
was passed out in a chair. Tex had shared the main image on
Facebook and some of the old crowd, now spread across the
world, liked the picture – but others untagged themselves.

Tex returned to Beirut after the war but soon was jailed
for possession of cannabis. When he got out of prison he
and Aida decided they needed a fresh start and moved to
the US. The marriage did not last, and when he returned to
Beirut in 2012, she didn't come with him.

Tex managed a small venue close to the Alley, where local
punks ran a soup kitchen, hang-out and language exchange
for Syrian refugees. But his landlord got sick of waiting
for the rent – he hadn't paid it in four months. Tex closed
the venue and moved to southern Lebanon, back to his
family home, to take up farming, his father's business. Still

jamming, Tex played with a new generation of metalheads who were children when the Hamra scene was at its peak. And he took pride in the fact that he has always fallen foul of the authorities: "I have been arrested more than 25 times, always for stupid things – being drunk, carrying knives and guns, drugs," he said. Bassem, who in the early 2000s had considered Tex, Ayat and the other Hamra bands his arch-enemies, admitted his respect: "Tex was true to himself. Of all people, he lived on the edge," he said.

Not everyone has been as loyal. A number of Tex's contemporaries on the Hamra scene have given up punk and black metal and have turned to God. The singer of Damaar is now a religious leader in Najaf, Iraq, and others have joined extreme Shia and Sunni movements. "We used to piss on mosques and burn Qurans and all this shit – just for the fuck of it," he said. "But more than 15 people in the group became extremists. Like extreme Shia sheikhs – they were even more radical than Hezbollah."

For Filthy Fuck, the conversion of many of the old crowd was particularly galling. He describes Damaar as his younger brothers, and when they went their separate ways and some turned to God, he found it hard to take.

I was distraught. Inconsolable. I loved those kids. And I could see it was going there. When I write a nice blasphemous line, I usually laugh to myself. I smile at the thought of how many people this will piss off. But the kids from Damaar actually hated God, and I always found that this was the wrong way to go about it. It destroys me to the core when I see people killing their talent because of fairy tales. It's nothing short of a tragedy. We lost some good men to religion.

Filthy Fuck recalled that a few months before Damaar disbanded, their drummer – who was also a guitarist and vocalist – was at his house, jamming songs that would be on a new album:

I told him, "This is the best metal I have ever heard. It will blow Ayat out of the water." I was listening to someone who perceived our records as the epitome of the genre which should be emulated. But he was far better than we could ever manage to be. What a shame. He's also somewhere being all Islamic and it just doesn't sit well with me at all. I feel like a preacher man who lost his kids to black metal.

For Safa, the loss of a close friend and bandmate to religion was equally acute but he has learned to accept it – even understand it. "I was in shock, of course, but got used to it later – maybe it was what he was really searching for through his extreme lifestyle. I guess he found it. Islam can be more extreme than black metal as a philosophy," he said.

Lydia has spread her message of co-existence and peace across the world. During 2014 and 2015 she addressed the United Nations on human rights issues on no fewer than five occasions. Three decades since she first took to the stage in Beirut, she is far better known for her activism than her music.

Malikah and Eslam Jawad both now live in Dubai, where she works in marketing and he runs a successful events management company. Both have had big success but are disappointed that the Lebanese hip hop scene has not achieved its potential. "We went a long way to pave the way for all those new rappers today. When we started there were no venues that would allow us to perform, no studios. We'd rap on the street or just use instrumentals. From that until today, when we tour around the world, we have everything we need – it's amazing," said Malikah. "But we need some Arabic hip hop you can play in a club – we don't have that."

For Eslam, the business case for Lebanese hip hop has still not been made. "Arabic hip hop is not a financially sustainable industry. I think that is partly due to us: we are very serious in terms of the things we talk about. There needs to be room for more fun stuff," he said.

As for Filthy Fuck, he left Beirut in 2014 after growing increasingly angry and erratic in Lebanon, culminating in his taking a beating in a mass brawl in the street outside his house. "I told my wife: if you don't want us dead, we need to leave," he said. Ayat released a second album, *Carry on Carrion*, in October 2016 but it was old material, recorded years earlier. It still crosses his mind that somebody will find out his real name or his home address and that there may be consequences for the things that Ayat have said. "I know plenty who'd be willing to plaster my name on a billboard if it could hurt me," he said. "When push comes to shove we'll probably have to answer for our decisions."

CHAPTER 2
IRAN

Meraj Ansari gripped the chain-link fence in the jail in Mashhad, north-eastern Iran, and waited for his lashes to begin. Behind him was the judge, who, hours earlier, had sentenced him to be flogged 100 times for satanism, standing next to a prison officer, a religious cleric and a group of soldiers. Meraj, a martial arts fanatic, knew he could handle the beating. He had made up his mind that those gathered would not hear him scream. "I was silent. I was relaxed. I was strong in front of those bastards," he said.

The prison officers wanted to handcuff him to the fence, so that when the flogging began he would not fall to the ground, but he refused. He insisted he could handle it. "I never screamed. I stayed strong." The first prison officer flogged him exactly 67 times, before handing over to his colleague, who gave him the other 33.

When his sentence was up, Meraj lowered his arms, but the judge insisted that many of the strokes of the whip had not been hard enough and that he should have 30 more. As he was beaten, the soldiers laughed and mocked him. On the other side of the fence was another prisoner, slumped on the concrete, forced to watch the ordeal as a form of psychological torture. When it finally finished, Meraj lowered his hands, put on his shirt, and looked at each of the men in turn. "They wanted to break me. All of them were shocked. I just looked at them, and I left," he said.

Outside the jail, his mother was waiting in the car and, seeing Meraj walking calmly out of the prison, assumed that he had managed to avoid the flogging, perhaps by paying off one of the guards. She insisted that he drove himself home. When he got back to the house and took off his shirt, his back and legs were bloody and raw.

That's when his mother began to scream.

It had been six months since Meraj's martial arts club and studio was raided in downtown Mashhad. He had used the studio as a recording space for Master of Persia, the heavy metal band fronted by his friend, Anahid. Meraj was charged with satanism and originally sentenced to 180 lashes and a fine of $4,000 before it was reduced to 100 lashes and $300 on appeal. In the six months between that sentence and his flogging in Mashhad, he had spent some time in the local jail until a relative of one of his students stumped up the cash for his bail.

For nine months after the beating, Meraj laid low, but one day a representative of the city's religious authorities called his father and demanded he report to the police station.

He didn't, and a few weeks later a well-connected student said that both Meraj and Anahid had been discussed during a high-level meeting of the city authorities. "They said we have music in this city and there is a group named Master of Persia. The girl has a shaved head and is a satanist," he said.

A prominent local religious leader, Ayatollah Alam Alhoda, told the meeting that the band members were kaffirs, or unbelievers, and demanded that the authorities deal with them. This, said Meraj, was serious. "When a big mullah says 'kaffir', this is no joke. They don't need the documents and the law – they will kill you," he said. Ayatollah Alhoda also had a history of such pronouncements: in 2012 he had called for an Iranian rapper, Shahin Najafi, in exile in Germany, to be assassinated. Najafi was later given a death sentence for apostasy by another hard-line cleric based in Qom, and an Iranian news website announced a $100,000 reward for anyone who killed him.

Within four days, Meraj had sold his car for $4,000 and he and Anahid had fled Iran, first travelling to Tehran and then across the border by bus. They have not been back since.

Meraj met Anahid when she was a student at his martial arts school in Mashhad in 2008. Meraj was a national champion in both jiu-jitsu and karate who had won both local and international championships. Many young men and women attended his school, including Anahid. When she was 18, Anahid joined Master of Persia.

Meraj had started the band three years earlier in 2005, and had already performed for friends at secret gigs in Mashhad, which, despite being deeply conservative, was home to a large heavy metal scene. Metal fans in the city would grow their hair long but tuck it into their T-shirts or jackets to avoid scrutiny from the religious authorities. They would also drive rather than walk the streets to avoid the attention of the police. "It was a risk. We had to hide ourselves from the eyes of the police. But the metalheads were brave hearts. They didn't care about the law," he said.

Every three months Meraj invited the various bands in Mashhad to jamming sessions at the secret music studio he had built at his martial arts school. He would call each person individually and instruct them to come only in groups of two or three. When they were nearby, they would call and he would let them in. "It often took hours to get everyone into the place – and then the same to get them all out again. Sometimes there were more than 100 people there," he said.

But the sessions were an invaluable way for the bands on the scene not only to form bonds but to share techniques and learn from each other. If anything, Meraj said, the risks that metalheads had to go through in Mashhad meant that the scene there and in wider Iran was far stronger than elsewhere in the region. "The Islamic system in Iran says that anyone who works in underground music is not only a satanist but a kaffir. With that kind of risk, I can say that we are more active and serious than other countries in the Middle East," he said.

If the risks were severe for Meraj and the other male members of the scene, they were far worse for Anahid. Her parents never supported her music and eventually threw her out of the house because of it.

Iran had a tradition of female musicians that stretched back for hundreds of years, but after the revolution of 1979, women were banned from singing live in the country. Shia clerics argued that the sound of a woman's voice aroused sexual feelings in men. The law was later changed to forbid women singing solo to men who were not related to them. In 2015, conservative cleric Hassan Nouri Hamedani specifically referenced the use of female vocals in music, arguing that it led to sexual arousal. "No action can normalise women's singing," he said. "We will stop it."

Female musicians in Iran risk not only jail but so-called 'honour attacks', particularly in a religious city like Mashhad: "There was the fear of arrest and imprisonment and even having acid thrown on the face or bodies of women who were active in music – even death in some cases," she said. "In my opinion, this is one of the biggest reasons that Iranian women are not that active in music, especially in heavy metal and rock."

Meraj and Anahid have lived in exile since 2012, but the risk from the authorities is so severe that they will not reveal where. They continue to play shows and record tributes to the bands that they grew up listening to, including Sepultura, and they have gained a huge following both inside and outside Iran.

While in recent years a number of stories have emerged of live shows being held in Tehran, Meraj dismisses them as a con: former president Ahmadinejad had promised to allow a cultural space to form in Iran when he was first elected in 2005, but once in power, he became one of the most authoritarian leaders the country has ever had. The live shows that have been held recently are part of the same process. Hassan Rouhani, Iran's current leader, may have a reputation as a reformer, but that does not mean that the country is on the road to reform. "They are just showing off, for social media, to say that we are free here. But the government is crazy – they can change their mind at any time."

Meraj is no longer active within Iran, but he keeps well briefed on the scene back home, and estimates that there are still over 1,700 active bands: "I am connected with many of them," he said.

* * *

In 2009, Obash Karampour, Koory Mirzeai, and brothers Soroush and Arash Farazmand arrived at the US embassy in Istanbul as part of their American visa application. The four men – who made up Iranian rock band Yellow Dogs –

had applied for permission to play a tour of US clubs before heading to Europe to promote *No One Knows About Persian Cats*, the Bahman Ghobadi film in which they had appeared earlier that year. It was a run-of-the-mill visa consultation, but officials took the opportunity to grill the well-spoken, English-speaking musicians about the burgeoning Green Movement and the street protests that had followed the 2009 elections, which had seen hard-line leader Mahmoud Ahmadinejad defeat reformist Hossein Mousavi.

The election was widely condemned as rigged, leading Iran's Supreme Leader, Ayatollah Ali Khamenei, to call for an investigation. But when the nation's Guardian Council upheld the decision, the protests picked up pace. On 4 November 2009, a public holiday that commemorates the 1979 takeover of the American embassy in Tehran, tens of thousands of Mousavi supporters took to the streets. On 7 December, Student Day in Iran, thousands turned out again. In the US and across Europe, there was a sense that the Green Movement could be winning – that it might lead to actual reform in Iran, which was then completely isolated from the international community and subject to a crippling oil embargo.

A day later, the four floppy-haired Iranian musicians piled into the US embassy for their interview.

Yellow Dogs had grown up during a brief period of social tolerance under Mohammad Khatami, the reformist president who held power between 1997 and 2005. Khatami had won 70 per cent of the vote when he ran in 1997 on a platform of change, rights for women and the rule of law. He had beaten the candidate backed by the Ayatollahs and became the figurehead for the reformist movement in Iran.

But from the earliest days of his presidency, Khatami was pestered by hard-line clerics. By 2004 he had been completely sidelined by Iran's parliament, but his short time in power had also seen the lifting of some social restrictions and more freedom of the press. Mousavi was seen as a tempering influence on the Ayatollahs, and he had a genuine following among well-educated, professional and secular (or at least less religious) Iranians.

The man who replaced him in 2005, Mahmoud Ahmadinejad, could not have been more different, and immediately began rolling back the slim reforms that Khatami had achieved. But by this point the die had been cast: Obash, Koory, Soroush and Arash had made the decision not to follow many of their peers into engineering or law, but to pursue music full time. Their parents, middle-class, educated and professional city-dwellers, supported their decision. Yellow Dogs was born.

The band's story has been told in various newspapers over the years, but it wasn't until WikiLeaks published leaked US diplomatic cables in December 2010 that the embassy transcripts came to light. In them, the unnamed US officials struggle to hide their fascination with the "astute, well-informed and resourceful 20-something" applicants and draw attention to their vivid description of a "small but crazy" underground club scene where "drugs are cheap and easy to find, creative expression is at its most free, and participants are among Iran's most tech-savvy citizens".

The drug of choice in Tehran was amphetamine, because it could be created synthetically in underground labs, although heroin and morphine were easy to find and not expensive. Despite the Islamic Republic's reputation for hard-line policies towards alcohol, drug users generally would not get jail time but instead were forced to attend clinics or to take medication.

Unfortunately, the authorities were not so progressive when it came to music, and all four of the band told of severe run-ins with the police. During one raid of their practice space, a member of the band was arrested and accused of worshipping Satan and was only released after two weeks of pleading by his parents and the payment of a bribe.

All of them had been arrested at one time or another over "style and clothing immoralities" and Koory had been forced to shave his huge brown afro after police took his driving licence and refused to give it back until he did so.

Yellow Dogs' first gig was held in the basement of a house in Tehran's western suburbs. The band had boarded up the windows and doors, and had friends looking out for the police because hundreds of young people were drinking, smoking and dancing inside. "We really had no idea what crime we were committing by playing music," Obash said. "At our concerts everything that was illegal was legal. Women didn't have to wear the veil, boys and girls were together, there was a dance floor. None of those people had ever been to a rock concert before."

The existence of the underground scene reflected the fact that there were two Irans, worlds apart when it came to values and orientation. On one side were those who lived in the cities, who were often well-educated and well-versed in both Persian poetry and western literature, and who travelled abroad often and watched satellite TV. This was Mousavi's and Khatami's world, one that saw Iran's future as being better integrated into the international community. On the other side was a far bigger rural population who were deeply religious, predominantly conservative and read little beyond government-controlled newspapers and the Quran. Many of them had never left Iran or even their own province; they had never used a computer, never watched a foreign film, had never heard of The Beatles. It was this world that the Ayatollahs relied on for support and that Ahmadinejad, who ran on a populist platform of social conservatism but also a fairer distribution of wealth to the poor, depended upon.

Yellow Dogs' basement venue survived for a while, but then had to be abandoned. "We did everything we could to avoid being seen," Karampour said. "But after our second show we heard that some neighbours were calling the cops, telling them that weird activity was going on. So we said, 'Fuck that. We are never playing here again.'" The band moved to a rooftop 'practice room' on the outskirts of Tehran, which is how they met Bahman Ghobadi, the acclaimed Kurdish-Iranian director of *A Time for Drunken Horses*. He featured Yellow Dogs in his award-winning film *Nobody Knows about Persian Cats*, a semi-fictional story of musicians struggling against censorship and repression in Tehran and dreaming of a life in the United States.

The film captures Yellow Dogs' passion for their music as well as their irreverent sense of humour – in one scene they are shown laughing at the absurdity of their situation when the young boy living opposite hears them playing their instruments and calls the police. In another, the band is seen playing their catchy, electro-tinged punk rock on the roof of a building with Tehran laid out before them and the mountains beyond. Yellow Dogs play only a small part in the movie, which centres on a couple, Negar and Ashkan, as they try to make plans to leave Iran and pursue a career in music in Europe. Along the way, they come across a number of bands, from rock and blues musicians to traditional Iranian folk singers, all of whom are unable to pursue music because of the strict Islamic rules against performing live that followed the 1979 revolution.

The film was a huge success outside Iran (where, unsurprisingly, it was banned), winning a Special Jury Prize at the 2009 Cannes Film Festival, but it also earned Yellow Dogs unwanted attention at home. Indeed, Ghobadi and most of his cast fled Iran in the wake of the film's release. "Suddenly the government became very interested in us," recalled Karampour.

> They made a TV series about musicians and said all these people are satanists and we have to execute all of them and that they don't believe in God. So after we saw that stuff and after the film we thought, "Man, we have to get out of the country before we get our asses busted."

A high-profile interview that same year on CNN made the band feel even more nervous, and when they arrived in Istanbul to play their first ever legal show, it was time to get serious. It was billed as a short-term trip, but they knew they were unlikely to be returning home. The band arranged their meeting at the US embassy and within a year all four members had received American visas, which meant that they could begin applying for political asylum. They rented a house in Brooklyn, where they lived with Ali Salehezadeh, who became their manager, and slipped into what was a well-established Iranian expatriate music scene in the US.

Those who came across the band were always interested in their background, but Yellow Dogs immediately began writing songs that referred to their new life, rather than their old. In 'This City', written soon after their arrival, Obash paints a picture of the carefree pace of life of a young 20-something living in New York. "Traffic lights, late at night, blinking to me / A sign of morning, I'm totally wasted, laying in her bed / She's smoking a cigarette, on the balcony / Am I alive or dead?"

Then, in December 2011, they were joined by their musician friends from Tehran, The Free Keys. The band had been unable to get a visa for their bassist, so they found a replacement: Mohammadi Rafie.

* * *

It often comes as a surprise that of all the metal scenes in the Middle East, Iran has produced the largest number of black metal bands. The popularity of the genre appears a contradiction given that Iran is one of only two countries in the region where blasphemy can land you a death sentence.

But while there are anti-religious bands from Iran, what has tended to attract Iranian metalheads to heavy metal's most extreme incarnation has not been its opposition to or denigration of religion, but rather its obsession with nature and ancient history. When Norway's Immortal sing about mythical worlds, frozen wastelands and endless, snow-covered forests, Iranians recognize the epic landscapes of their own homeland.

Likewise, just as countless black metal bands from Scandinavia have drawn on the legends of the Vikings, so Iranian musicians have sought to draw influences from the thousands of years of Persian history, with its vast empires, warring kings and pre-Islamic mythology. Master of Persia are, at their roots, a classic death metal band, but just as their heroes Sepultura drew influences from the tribal music of Brazil, so Meraj and Anahid use traditional instruments and themes from Persian mythology as the basis for their songs, written in their own language.

For Meraj, that obsession with Iran and its history makes his exile all the more painful. He believes clerics and corrupt politicians who have taken over Iran since the 1979 revolution have no more right to what is Iranian than Meraj, yet it is he that has had to leave. In their song 'Prince of Persia', Anahid sings of this forbidden, pre-Islamic Iran: "Shame to the day that man / Doesn't learn from the history of the past."

Sina Winter grew up listening to black metal bands Burzum and Mayhem and found similarities with the freezing Norwegian landscapes that they described in his native Iran in winter, when snow would cap the mountains that surround his home city of Tehran. He founded a one-man black metal band, From the Vastland, and began writing music that captured not just the scenery of Iran, but its mythology. Sina composed songs about the many gods of Persia and the battle between good and evil that is the basis of ancient Persian and Zoroastrian thought. His first release as From the Vastland was the song 'Darkness vs Light: The Perpetual Battle'. He looked abroad, to Norway, for his musical influences but looked to home when writing lyrics. "Iran has this background, not just because of the nature but because of the history. It is perfect for black metal music," he said.

But while Iran's rich history may be perfect for black metal, its culture since the revolution of 1979 isn't. Iran's religious authorities rejected not only the pre-Islamic themes of Sina's music but the harsh, heavy sound of black metal. They were also sophisticated enough to know the age-old link between metal – and particularly black metal – and satanism.

Iranian bands were rarely anti-religious and almost never satanic, Sina said. "Most bands were talking about the general black metal topics. The lyrics were about darkness, forests, nature. They were not into satanism. But, of course, the government and religious people, they gave this name to metal musicians – they called it satanic, blasphemous or whatever." In a religious theocracy where blasphemy is illegal, it was a dangerous path to tread.

Sina and a friend quickly adopted the fashion of heavy metal, growing their hair long and sewing onto their jackets the patches and band logos that their friends would buy from overseas. But there was little or no organised scene in the country in the 1990s. "There was no internet, no record shops, no labels, no scene – nothing. It was really hard to find metal tapes – our only source was people who were going abroad and bringing them back," he said.

Sina formed his first band, Sorg Innkalleise, in 2003 with his cousin and recorded two albums which they began to distribute among other metal fans they knew in Tehran. As the CDs got passed around, word got back to Sina and his cousin that there was a hot new Norwegian band, Sorg Innkalleise, that was making great music. He didn't put anyone right for three years. To this day, he finds that those who don't know From the Vastland assume that he is Norwegian when they hear his music. "I like that," he said.

One of Sina's first influences was one-man black metal outfit Burzum, probably the most controversial band in the global heavy metal scene due to the political views and actions of its founder, Varg Vikernes, who was jailed in 1994 for the murder of Mayhem guitarist Euronymous. Vikernes, who openly flirts with white nationalism, is reviled by all but a tiny portion of the global black metal scene but his early music has been a seminal influence for many bands.

Over the fuzz of guitars, ambient soundscapes and blast beats, Vikernes' high-pitched shrieks are like a soundtrack to a journey to the pits of hell. When Sina first heard Burzum's 1993 album *Filosofem* on a cassette smuggled into Iran by a friend, he was hooked.

But from the beginning it was a challenge for Sina to learn to play the fast, tremolo-picking riffs of black metal and harder still to develop the harsh growling vocals that are so integral to the genre. He had a guitar teacher early on, but he was unable to show him what he wanted to know. He ended up learning by listening to albums again and again. "When I started the screaming I had no idea how to do it and it hurt. But after a short time of trying you understand how to do it without it hurting," he said.

Like many artists in Tehran, Sina had his own studio and the band locked themselves away for hours, trying to perfect the stark Norwegian sound that he first heard through Burzum. He began swapping Sorg Innkalleise CDs with other bands, and getting positive feedback from other Iranian metallers. But they also started getting their first threats from religious groups. The warnings began as emails or text messages and Sina considered them pretty harmless until he got his first death threat. "They said they knew us and they would find us and execute us," he said.

The mid-2000s had been a period of openness in Iran. Mohammed Khatami was in power and for two or three years it was possible to organise metal shows, despite the anger of the religious authorities. But these were not metal shows in the normal sense. In order to get a permit, bands had to agree to stringent restrictions on what could be done at gigs, both on and off the stage. "They had to play the shows without vocals and the audience had to sit down. It was usually in a cinema or an amphitheatre and the authorities would check people didn't headbang – but still at least they could play the show," he said.

By this point he estimates that there were between 10 and 15 active bands in Iran, mostly death metal and thrash, and at least three playing black metal. Then, in 2005, Ahmadinejad took power: "It stopped with Ahmadinejad. They started to ban everything – for a short while it was not possible to play any kind of rock music or even release instrumental albums," he said.

The underground scene continued to organise shows despite the new hard-line government in Tehran. Sina played two shows in Tehran in recording studios owned and operated by fellow musicians, but it was too risky to have more than 20 people in attendance. It was not uncommon for even these small studio gigs to be raided by the police, and at least one of his friends was arrested and forced to close his studio. On other occasions, even if the police stayed away, religious vigilantes would often turn up at an advertised show and close it down, acting on the orders of local clerics. "They give permits for live concerts but, right when they want to play, some authorities or religious groups would come and close the venue, arrest people and take their instruments," Sina said.

In 2010, Sina formed From the Vastland and signed a record deal with an independent Norwegian label. He was invited to Norway for the first time to perform at Inferno Festival in Oslo alongside musicians from Gorgoroth, 1349 and Morbid Angel, some of the biggest bands in the genre. "I was a bit stressed even just knowing I was going to play with them. But they were friendly and I calmed down and I was sure everything would be OK. We had the biggest crowd at Inferno that day," he said.

But as Sina began performing overseas, he also began getting attention from the authorities, especially after he was interviewed on the BBC, which was then banned in Iran. He managed to get a cultural visa to study in Norway and has not been back to Iran since.

Gone are the days when the religious police didn't know the difference between black metal and death metal, between what is an irreligious genre and what is essentially more light-hearted and tongue in-cheek, he said. In their efforts to suppress the scene in Iran, the authorities have become experts in it. "I know even if I go back to Iran I will get serious problems. I am sure that they know about me," he said.

While Sina does not consider his music either irreligious or political, he is aware that just by being a black metal musician from Iran, he *is* political. "I am not into politics. But when you come from a country like Iran and you are playing black metal music, a lot of people look at you as if you have a political message as well. Because you are fighting for something," he said.

> But I am fighting for freedom of my art; it isn't
> about politics, it is about art. To me, music is the
> most important thing, and I am fighting for that.
> I am bringing this message. But since I am in Iran,
> I think people think there is a political message.

Even if Hassan Rouhani has tried to make Iran a more open country since he was elected – agreeing a historic deal with the US and Europe to end sanctions on Iran in return for the country shelving its nuclear programme – the religious authorities still hold sway. "People expect me to say that Iran has become more open now when it comes to relations with Europe and the nuclear deal, but it isn't true. This is something that you just hear or see in the media; what is going on inside the country is very different," Sina said.

In Norway, Sina Winter has blended into his adopted country and been successful as a musician. But it has not been easy being an immigrant from the Middle East. He initially came to the country on a two-year cultural visa arranged by the director of a film, *Blackhearts*, about heavy metal in Iran and other unusual countries and then got a job working as an editor in a video production company.

But things are harder as rhetoric tightens against immigrants in post-migrant-crisis Europe – even in Scandinavia. Sina has to renew his visa every six months and finds it impossible to make long-term plans as he never knows if he will be allowed to stay. "It is not easy to manage your life when everything is uncertain," he said. He wants to stay in Norway and continue touring and learning. He has recently worked with musicians from bands such as 1349 and Destructor, and when *Blackhearts* comes out it can only be a good thing for his profile. He was a black metal musician for 12 years in Iran before coming to Norway, and he isn't ready to leave. "I have learned a lot working in this professional scene. Here in Norway, black metal is really serious. It is actually popular here. Everything is official. It is a completely different world," he said.

* * *

On 5 October 2013, Iran's feared Revolutionary Guards raided an office in the northern Iranian city of Sari, in the province of Mazandaran, where three men – Hossein Rajabian, his brother Mehdi Rajabian and their friend Yousef Emadi – were working. They shot all three with a stun gun and then blindfolded them and drove them to the local police headquarters, where they were tortured, and then drove them to Tehran's notorious Evin Prison, home to most of Iran's political prisoners.

At Evin, the three men were taken to solitary confinement and threatened with life in jail if they did not make video confessions. Finally, in December 2013, they were released on bail. In 2015, the three men were finally convicted of "insulting Islamic sanctities", "spreading propaganda against the system" and "illegal audio-visual activities" that stemmed from Mehdi's work as a musician and Hossein's as a filmmaker and sentenced to five years in prison. They appealed, but after a 45-minute hearing in June 2016 they were told that they would serve at least three years in jail. As of early 2017, jail was where Mehdi, Yousef and Hossein remained.

Amnesty International has branded the treatment of the men as "grossly unfair", pointing out that their initial trial lasted only three minutes. The charges related to Hossein's feature film, *The Upside-down Triangle*, which documents women's right to divorce in Iran and Medhi's setting up of the site Barg Music, which distributes Persian-language music from artists outside the country. The site always had issues, but in 2012 it attracted attention when it distributed music by rapper Shahin Najafi, whose song about Shia religious figure Ali al-Hadi al-Naqi saw him branded an apostate. By this point, Barg Music had 300,000 visitors per day. Mehdi had been recording an album of Iranian music and when his studio was raided the police took all of his hard drives and instruments. Commenting on the case, Grand Ayatollah Hassan Nouri Hamedani said: "We will stop any film, book or music that is anti-Islamic and anti-revolutionary."

Mehdi and Youssef's conviction in June 2016 came just months after Rouhani signed a landmark deal with the US and Europe to ignore Iran's nuclear programme in return for the end of three decades of crippling sanctions imposed by the West. The deal was presented as a new era for Iran, and the country was able to begin exporting oil soon after it came into force. It was argued that it would not only open up Iran's economy but lead to greater freedom for its 77 million people.

A month later, the news broke that an Iranian death metal band, Confess, had been jailed for blasphemy. The case of Nikan Siyanor Khosravi, 23, and Arash Ilkhani, 21, had been highlighted by a Canadian metal DJ, Trev McKendry, who had known the band for a number of years after playing their music on his radio show. They were also charged with owning an independent record label and communicating with a foreign radio station – McKendry's Metal Nation.

The case of Confess was a warning: the nuclear deal may provide for Iran to open its economy to the world, but strict Islamic rule remained.

Confess had reached out to many of the Iranian bands since their formation in 2012. Sina remembered getting a message from them in 2014, just after they had released their new album and had been played on Metal Nation. He was shocked about what happened, but felt it could have been a great deal worse. Confess were lucky that their story got picked up by newspapers across the world, which probably persuaded the authorities not to go too far in punishing them. "To me, their music was not anti-religious or anything. They play Slipknot-style new wave metal music. They were not into politics or religion, but just because they are playing metal music the government makes problems with them," he said.

Meraj from Master of Persia also remembers being in touch with Confess back in 2012, when he and Anahid set up a festival for Iranian bands in Istanbul. They had wanted Confess on the bill, but they were still very young and did not have passports to travel to Turkey. He said that a recent track that touched on the Green Movement was probably the reason for their arrest: "Everyone knows that is a red line for the Islamic regime," he said.

On Confess's latest album, song titles included 'Teh-Hell-Ran' and 'I Am Your God Now', both of which were brave statements for a country like Iran. Their music is traditional new wave thrash metal: fast, tight and scuzzy. In the tradition of Sepultura and others, they use their music to hit out at government and religious authorities, and although they sing in English, their song names alone are enough to rile the Iranian authorities.

McKendry, 50, knew little about Iran until Nikan, Confess's singer, contacted him by email in 2012 and asked him to play a couple of their songs. He was in regular contact with the young man until last year, when he stopped getting emails. A few months later, a friend of the band got in touch to tell him what had happened. "I said I would do whatever I can," he said. Since then, he has become an expert on the Islamic Republic. He was sent court documents by the friend of the band and has had them translated from Farsi. He has also released the band's album, *The Last One Standing*, on SoundCloud after being sent the tracks prior to their arrest.

For McKendry, who has championed a number of Middle Eastern bands on his radio show, the case of Confess not only highlights the difficulties metal bands have in places such as Iran, but feeds into the concept that his show, Metal Nation, has always tried to spread: of unity. "It's not people, it is the governments that are creating this division between people," he said.

That is the concept behind Metal Nation. I don't care what sex you are, what language you speak, I don't care what colour your skin is, I don't care what your religion is or if you are gay or straight – if you love heavy metal, come on in. You're welcome.

The arrests do not chime with the new, free Iran that was supposed to follow the nuclear deal, but for those both inside and outside the country, that is not a surprise. Just as Yellow Dogs had told US officials in 2009, there was a huge difference between the Iran of the political elites like Rouhani and the clerics, who openly defied the President regularly in the wake of the nuclear deal.

In August 2016, Ahmad Alamolhoda, who once called for Anahid and Meraj from Master of Persia to be put to death, refused to allow singers to perform in Mashhad. Ali Jannati, Rouhani's Minister for Culture and Islamic Guidance, rolled over almost immediately, arguing that since the city was home to a significant Shia shrine, it was not appropriate for music to be performed live in the city.

At the end of September of the same year, hard-liners were outraged when a concert was held in Qom, south of Tehran and home to another important Shia shrine, forcing the city's Culture Ministry director to apologise. These were not heavy metal shows – they were not even western – but traditional Farsi music performed by men and women, with the latter wearing the hijab.

Much of the issue facing musicians in Iran is that concerts are not actually illegal. In order to play, musicians must get permission from the Ministry of Culture and Islamic Guidance, which will often request CDs of the bands in question and Farsi translations of the lyrics. The ministry may then permit the show to go ahead with certain caveats, such as a limit on the number of songs or a requirement that the bands do not have vocals.

Pouria Kamali, vocalist in Iranian band Dawn of Rage, managed to secure an elusive permit in 2012 for the band's third show in Iran. As in the past, Pouria had been told that, as the band was heavy metal, they could perform only one or two songs with vocals and the rest had to be instrumental, and that even the vocals had to be soft – they could not growl in the tradition of bands that had influenced their music, such as Lamb of God, Meshuggah and Gojira.

An hour before the show was due to start, the police showed up and accused Pouria of not having permission to organise the gig, as well as making allegations that the band and their fans were doing something far more dangerous – worshipping the devil. They stripped members of the crowd in order to inspect them for 'devil worship tattoos', confiscated mobile phones and photographed those who were released. Pouria and the rest of the band were thrown in prison. "They arrested everyone because of devil worshiping and metal music and blah blah. So the band went to jail for a couple of days," he said. But despite the arrests being fairly run-of-the-mill in a country like Iran, the charges were serious for Pouria. He and the rest of the band were able to post bail but he knew that, when he stood trial, he would be unlikely to escape jail time. He was active in the scene and regularly organised shows, not only for his own band. That was when he decided to head to Iran's border with Turkey and leave his home country forever.

It isn't just heavy metal bands that have found little changed in post-nuclear-deal Iran. Erfan Paydar, an Iranian rapper currently in exile in California, said that the same applies to Iran's underground hip hop scene. Iranian rappers are free to apply to the Ministry of Culture and Islamic Guidance, but the ministry will reject hip hop outright because it is considered 'western' music. "There is nothing that says rap music is illegal. But when you go to get permits they say you can't get it. You can't appeal it and you can't change that," he said.

Back in the 1990s, hip hop was not popular in Iran and few people were rapping in English, let alone in Farsi. Iranians could only access US hip hop via satellite television, but as dishes were illegal they had to be bought on the black market or smuggled into the country. From time to time the authorities would crack down on satellite dishes, which had to be mounted outside and were difficult to conceal, but whenever they were confiscated they would usually appear again later on illicit market stalls.

Satellite TV brought the music of Nas, Tupac, 50 Cent and Eminem into tens of thousands of Iranian homes, but it was the internet that gave birth to Persian hip hop. Young rappers were suddenly able to download instrumental tracks by American rappers, and then record Farsi lyrics over the top. The sound was ropey – as were the words – but it was a start. "There was a huge wave of rappers recording low quality, both in recording and lyrics, stuff at home over famous instrumentals," Erfan said.

Growing up in Iran, it was difficult not to be involved in politics. Erfan is 33 and many of his family and their friends remember Iran prior to 1979, when Tehran was a hub for music in the Middle East and was renowned for its party scene. "You'd hear all around from adults talking about how it was before the revolution," he said. Erfan contrasts that with the Iran of the 1990s, when musicians, artists and writers were regularly going to jail. "Stuff happened every day. So if you had any interest in politics, there was a lot to go around," he said. The fact that music had to be so underground, Erfan said, meant that it was impossible to make a living out of it, lending it an authenticity that remains today. "In a lot of ways, because there is no money to be made from it – that's what is beautiful about Iranian music," he said.

Erfan's debut album, *Az Khaaneh Taa Goor*, tackled life both in Iran and as an Iranian in the US. He collaborated with two other Iranian rappers, Khashayar and Afra, and toured the US, Canada, Sweden and the UK. 'Tasmin', a song dedicated to the then growing Green Movement, is the reason Erfan cannot return to Iran – although, like Sina, he has not been officially banned. "I really want to. I have been working on it for years. My struggle has been I haven't been able to get an answer. People have said my name and said I am on a couple of different lists of people who get in trouble," he said. "But the detail of it – I don't know. Would I go to jail? Or would they interview me? That's been the issue – I can't get a straight answer out of them."

After 15 years in the US, Erfan remains in awe of the size and breadth of an Iranian scene that has survived against the most difficult of odds. He has American-Iranian friends who return to Tehran often and are afraid to attend underground gigs. "But the people from Iran, they don't care. They're used to it. They're just looking forward," he said.

Erfan has his own label and has signed a few emerging Iranian rappers, while the underground scene has ballooned. "There are so many underground rappers trying to make a name for themselves. It is a really authentic scene. They are young and emotional and they have a big drive. But there are certain subjects they know not to touch. They don't want to go to jail."

Despite this growing scene, Erfan is pessimistic about political change leading to social freedom in Iran. He is old enough to remember the buzz that surrounded Khatami in the late 1990s, but, almost 20 years later, little has changed. "It never really happens. I have lived inside and outside of Iran my whole life. I've seen this happen over and over. The real change never really comes. It is good that people have hope but I think that is all it is," he said.

* * *

On 11 November 2013, Brooklyn musician Michael Vallarelli was at his desk early, reading through the headlines online when news began to break about a shooting involving a local band. "I immediately got chills," he recalled. "I had a feeling I would know the band. When I read it was them, I was completely shocked."

The news was that four young men were dead, two of them brothers Arash and Soroush Farazmand, the 28-year-old drummer and 27-year-old guitarist in Yellow Dogs. The third victim, 35-year-old Ali Eskandarian, was a friend, fellow musician and housemate. The shooter, who ultimately turned his gun on himself, was named as Mohammadi Rafie, a disgruntled musician who had been thrown out of The Free Keys a year earlier. Two members of Yellow Dogs – guitarist Obash Karampour and bassist Koory Mirzeai – weren't at home that night and survived the shooting.

When they had arrived in Brooklyn four years earlier, Yellow Dogs had not marketed themselves as an Iranian band. They didn't sing about politics and they didn't play protest music. In their interview at the US embassy, three out of the four admitted they had not taken part in the Green Movement protests. Karampour, the one member who had, said he had done so because he could not stay at home while his parents marched.

In the US, they didn't want to talk about Iran, feeling that there was more to them than their nationality and backstory. In interview after interview, the band members brushed off questions about politics but interviewers couldn't help but mention the women who flocked to their shows in contrast to the separation of the sexes they knew from home. But Yellow Dogs had attracted unwanted attention in Iran not because of what they sang about, but because they sang at all.

In Brooklyn they rehearsed and refined their sound – a danceable mix of hard rock, punk and funk. In promo videos for songs such as 'This City' and 'Dancefloor', the quartet's excitement to be in New York is palpable. In a film for music download service eMusic, the dreadlocked Karampour explained how they still couldn't believe they had achieved what friends in Iran used to dismiss as a crazy fantasy – to live and make music in New York. "If we were born in London or Los Angeles, it wouldn't be that exciting for us," he said. "But right now we appreciate everything. If we think about what we've been through, where we're from, and where we're playing now … it's joy and adrenaline."

Life in New York was good. They became friends with bands such as Nada Surf and Black Lips, whom they supported at Webster Hall and had long cited as an influence.

They were regular performers at South by Southwest, a vast music industry conference and festival in Austin, Texas, and in 2012 they performed with Phone Home at New York's famous Mercury Lounge. It was their biggest home-town show to date. "Yellow Dogs loved the Brooklyn music scene and they were loved by the scene," said Vallarelli. "Kids would dance non-stop during their sets and they brought so many people to their shows. Lots of Iranian kids attended but a fair mix of others did too."

Kevin Diamond, a 30-year-old singer and guitarist for the band Shark? played alongside Yellow Dogs twice in 2013. "They were just another Brooklyn band trying to make it," he recalled.

> It didn't seem strange to me that these guys were from Iran. They were just another group of dudes who were escaping a shitty home town to move somewhere they thought would be more supportive of their art. They came to Brooklyn for the same reason we all did. You can be who you want here.

In the summer of 2013, Arash was finally granted asylum and Yellow Dogs could start thinking about an overseas tour. Iran wasn't an option so they hoped to play in Istanbul, where they could meet family and friends from home. Then, in late 2013, Mohammadi Rafie went on his rampage.

Rafie had been dropped by Yellow Dogs' friends The Free Keys in May 2012 over both musical differences and accusations he had stolen money from his bandmates. It was reported that he had started sending death threats to other members of the band and posted a picture on Facebook of a .318 calibre assault rifle writing: "I've become a westerner."

On the night of the shootings, he had scrambled across the roof of a neighbouring building with a semi-automatic rifle he kept stashed in a guitar case and 100 rounds of ammunition. Once he climbed onto the terrace of Yellow Dogs' house, he moved from floor to floor, shooting everyone he came across. He shot Eskandarian dead through a third-floor window, and killed Soroush and Arash in their bedrooms. He shot a fourth person in the leg before climbing to the roof and shooting himself in the head. Karampour was at work in a local club when he received a call in the early hours from a friend. "I said: 'What is this, a prank?'" he told *Rolling Stone* after the shooting. He began to call the house that the band had shared in East Williamsburg but nobody was answering.

Within hours, the shootings had made international headlines, including in Iran. The international press clamoured for statements from the remaining two members of the band; fans and friends shared their music. A week later a tribute gig was held at the Brooklyn Bowl, headlined by their friends Nada Surf. In a moving statement, Obash and

Koory spoke of their utter disbelief at what had happened. They said that Ali Eskandarian, their friend, had almost finished his novel and that Arash had finally been given political asylum in the US. How everything they had worked for had finally come true. How the future seemed so bright.

> We are left with pain, emptiness and so many questions that won't ever be answered. We wanted the world to discover us as we were: a community of musicians defined by our music. This is not the way we ever imagined the world would learn of our story.

* * *

From time to time, there is news of new heavy metal shows in Iran. There are posts on social media, reports in local newspapers, and blogs or pictures on Instagram. There is talk of a thriving electronica scene in Tehran, with shows held in disused bunkers and warehouses as well as vast raves in the middle of the desert.

But most of the musicians who have the option of leaving Iran have done so. Sina has found peace in his tiny village on the outskirts of Trondheim, Norway. He is a ten-minute walk from a forest in one direction and fifteen minutes from a fjord in the other. As he walks around this frozen landscape, he is occasionally reminded of the snow-capped mountains that surround Tehran. "It was a big contrast, coming from a city of 12 million people, but I love it," Sina said. "Everywhere there is nature. The people are nice. It is great." But life is not without its challenges. Like many Middle East musicians, Sina is in Norway on an artist's visa that regularly needs renewing, and every time is like starting from scratch. It has not escaped his – or any exile's – attention that the tide of opinion in Europe is turning. The tragedy in Syria has led tens of thousands to come to Europe, and feelings are hardening against refugees – which is, effectively, what Sina is. Luckily he is surrounded by fellow musicians from Norway and elsewhere in Europe who believe in him and his music. Sina can rest easy – for now.

Other exiles have been more painful. Meraj's scars are not only the ones on his back and his legs from the lashes he received for his alleged satanism, but his anger with having his country taken from him. He and Anahid are out of Iran now but their hearts remain there. Master of Persia play festivals alongside internationally renowned bands and get thousands of views for their videos, particularly Anahid's pitch-perfect covers of songs by Sepultura and Cannibal Corpse. In 2015, they released their first music video for their song 'Mazda Huu' after they were featured in a documentary, *Rebel Music*, on MTV, which also featured Erfan.

But when Iran comes up, Meraj's bitterness comes to the fore. Many of those who have left Saudi Arabia or Egypt

– or even Israel – talk with a weary contempt about their country. They complain about its values, its lack of culture or its immaturity. Yellow Dogs had to leave Iran but they *wanted* to forget it; they didn't want to be known forever as an Iranian band. But for Meraj and Anahid, Master of Persia are Iranian; Iran is where they belong. Those soldiers who laughed at Meraj as he was being beaten never got to see him scream. They couldn't take his pride, and the mullahs will not take his country either. If the Islamic Republic were to collapse tomorrow, Anahid and Meraj would be on the first plane to Mashhad.

Erfan's exile has not been easy either. It began just three years after his arrival in the US, in 2001, when al-Qaeda flew two commercial airliners into the World Trade Center in New York, killing almost 3,000 people and changing the world forever. In the days and weeks following the attack, over 1,200 people, most of them Arab Muslims, were rounded up by police and immigration officials and detained for anything between a few hours to weeks. In the chaos that followed the attacks, the US authorities ordered that all Lebanese, Syrian and Iranian nationals over the age of 16 report to their local police station for an interview, and Erfan, then 19, complied. "I went in for the interview and they talked to me for barely five minutes before they arrested me," he said. He was kept at the police station until 5 am before being transferred to the city jail.

Over the next three weeks, Erfan saw the inside of at least three different jails, including a maximum security prison where guards would hose the inmates down naked. During interviews, Erfan would plead with officials to consider that not a single Iranian national was involved in the 9/11 attacks, but they would not listen. "They treated us like shit. We hadn't done anything, no crime." he said. Erfan was eventually released, but, like many of those detained following 9/11, he was fighting deportation in the courts for years and his case was only resolved in 2006. "It was very tough on me then and in the years to come and I would get stressed, worried and defensive every time I saw police instead of feeling safe," he said.

At 33, Erfan has now spent as much time living in the US as he had in Iran, and yet he feels a stranger to both cultures. He sings in Farsi and his fans are Iranians, yet he lives in California, playing music invented in America. But then he was always sandwiched between these two worlds. "In Iran I was the Iranian kid from America and when I was in America I was just the Iranian kid," he said. These experiences have made him challenge what it is to leave your country for somewhere completely different – to be a stranger, an immigrant, in someone else's land. It has become a major theme in his music, and something that his fans constantly get in touch to comment on. As Erfan said:

When you're in Iran there is a picture of moving outside and migrating to America that is so rosy. You think everything is going to be great as soon as I go there. I'm going to have a great life and make a lot of money. I'm going to be so free. And then when you come here you see that, no, there are a lot of challenges. I've had messages and emails from fans that said, when I lived in Iran, I liked this song but I didn't really get it. Now that I have moved away it makes so much sense. I see the struggle. I see it isn't easy.

CHAPTER 3
EGYPT

On 5 June 2016, in the front room of a private villa on the outskirts of Cairo, Brazilian thrash metal veterans Sepultura were due to play when the police swarmed in. The officer in charge approached Egyptian-American organiser Nader Sadek and accused him of failing to get a permit for the show. Then he asked him for a bribe. When Nader refused to pay up, the police arrested him, his sound engineer and the owner of the villa. They were driven to a police station downtown, where they were interrogated and then thrown in the cells. It was a week before anyone heard from Nader again.

The media later reported that Nader had failed to get the relevant permissions to host the show, but the head of Egypt's state-backed musicians syndicate, Hany Shaker, alluded to something more sinister. The crowd had been "dressed in a very strange style and drew their make-up in the shape of a pentagram," he told local newspaper *Al-Ahram*. They also "wore leather jackets with stars on the back".

His comments had worrying echoes for older heavy metal fans in Egypt who remembered the media witch-hunt in 1997 that led to a bloody crackdown, mass arrests and the jailing of dozens of young men. It was not the first time that Shaker, a 63-year-old pop star, had set his sights on Egypt's metal scene: in February 2016 he had told al-Assema TV that the syndicate had shut down two "satanist parties" in Cairo. It later emerged that, despite that action, a third concert organised by Nader had taken place that night featuring a satanic black metal band from Colombia, Inquisition.

Nader was born and raised in Cairo but lived in New York for more than a decade before he returned to Egypt just after the 2011 revolution. After organising a successful run of gigs by international acts in Cairo, he had finally brought Sepultura to the country.

Sepultura are an important band for metalheads across the world, but in Egypt after the Arab Spring their raw, political thrash metal was starkly relevant. The band rose out of the slums of Belo Horizonte, Brazil, in the early 1980s when the country was run by its own brutal military dictatorship, and they went on to become one of the most important heavy metal bands of their generation. Founded by brothers Igor and Max Cavalera, their anger towards the corruption, nepotism and poverty of Brazil found its voice in the ferocity of thrash. Bands from all four corners of the globe have tried to imitate their sound since then, but

Sepultura's background gave their music an authenticity that could never be matched by middle-class kids from the US or Europe. Speaking to a US newspaper journalist in 1993, Max Cavalera said: "Traveling on trains. Getting beat up by cops. Sleeping behind the stage … It's part of the nature of this stuff. If you don't have that kind of background, you can't be a band like us."

In 'Refuse/Resist', Sepultura's call-to-arms anthem, Cavalera wrote "Chaos AD / Tanks on the streets / Confronting police / Bleeding the plebs" about the protests against military dictatorship in Brazil. In 2011, such words had resonance for young Egyptians on the streets of Cairo and the song became an anthem for those from the metal community involved in the revolution.

In 2016, those heady days may have felt like a distant memory but there was still huge anticipation about the show on the Egyptian music scene. For decades, metalheads in Egypt had been hampered by government crackdowns and the fact that Sepultura – whose songs call for resistance and revolution and take aim at governments, elites and the police – could play in Cairo was seen as evidence that the decades of struggle by the Egyptian scene was bearing fruit.

In the days and weeks following the aborted Sepultura show, some argued that the issue had been about permits or the last minute change of venue from Cairo's Nile Country Club to a more secluded private residence in Sheikh Zayed.

There was a perception that while the cancellation of the show was unfortunate, it was not emblematic of a renewed crackdown: rival promoters blamed Nader personally for just simply not having his shit together. But scene veterans knew better. "It was a message," said one, before sharing a picture on Facebook that showed an armoured personnel carrier and several other police vehicles surrounding the villa: "You think they needed all those cops for a permit violation?"

A week later Nader took to Facebook to reveal that he had been acquitted of two charges, one a permit violation and the other promoting blasphemy, or, as it is enshrined in Egyptian law: 'contempt for religion'. The charge is one that has been levied often since 2011, targeting poets, writers and artists as well as musicians, and can carry a five-year prison sentence.

Nader had escaped jail, but his week in police custody had been no picnic. When he arrived the guards tossed him into a packed cell and told the other prisoners that he was a Satan worshipper: "I guess they hoped they would beat me or rape me or whatever," he said. Whether it was because his fellow prisoners hated the cops more than they hated satanists, or the fact that Nader entertained his cell-mates by singing death metal songs acapella, he wasn't harmed. He was finally dragged before the court after four days and legally vindicated, but the police threw him back in prison for another three days instead of letting him go. When he argued with the guards, one of them put a lit cigarette out on his foot.

As far as Middle East metal scenes go, Egypt is one of the strongest – but it is also one of the most harassed. Cairo and Alexandria may be cosmopolitan, liberal and relatively diverse cities, but much of the rest of the country adheres to the strict, pious Islam of the Muslim Brotherhood and the ultraconservative Salafi faith. Egypt gave birth to some of the Arab world's most progressive and liberal voices and was at the heart of the Middle East music and film industry for decades. But it also produced Sayyid Qutb, the Egyptian author and Brotherhood member whose writings inspired a generation of fanatics from Osama bin Laden to ISIS. Egyptian rulers from Gamal Abdul Nasser in the 1950s to Abdel Fattah el-Sisi today have contained the Muslim Brotherhood but they have also had to mollify generations of clerics and the pious by appearing to be good Islamic leaders.

Egypt's metalheads have often proved to be useful sacrificial lambs for both the police and politicians, and the Egyptian media has often been happy to wield the knife. Just as the spate of church burnings and murders that outraged Norway in the 1990s brought black metal into the mainstream consciousness in Europe, so stories of seances and lurid debauchery at underground metal shows in Cairo provided fodder for the state-owned Egyptian press. Music syndicate chief Shaker may be hated by all but a handful of musicians in Egypt, but his stories fill column inches and airtime for Middle East TV stations just as stories of sex and celebrity do elsewhere.

After he graduated, Nader worked as an artist in New York, where his work was focused on the duality of his heritage. Like many who make their homes in a foreign land, he was interested in issues of cultural identity. His 2007 exhibition *Faceless* drew on the fact that, while in Cairo he was attacked as a devil worshipper because of his tattoos and piercings, in the US he could not escape being seen as an Arab, and therefore dangerous. His love of death metal marked him out as a threat in the country of his birth, while the country of his birth marked him out as a threat in America.

His work was not always directly about music. It also included elements of performance art, such as his taking to the streets of New York in traditional Arab dress and documenting how differently he was treated compared with when he wore western garb. But death metal's influence was integral to all of Nader's early work as an artist. "I'm an artist, not a musician. All my art and all my sculptures and exhibitions have always been connected to death metal somehow. Even back then my ideas were about resistance to common thought," he said.

As a genre, death metal has always been designed to shock, to provoke reaction, both in its lyrics and in its flat-out brutal sound, epitomised by low-tuned guitars, fast-picked riffs and lightning-quick drumming. The lyrics, performed in a low growl, depict violence and murder, misanthropy, cannibalism and mutilation. Death metal bands such as Deicide – whose songs include 'When Satan Rules the World' – and Cannibal Corpse ('Fucked With a Knife' and 'Meat Hook Sodomy') have been banned from multiple countries, upsetting everyone from Christians to animal rights activists.

Bands on the death metal scene are often criticised – fairly, many would argue – for their glamorisation of violence, particularly given that it often targets women ('Stripped, Raped and Strangled' is another prominent Cannibal Corpse song). Musicians and fans contend that death metal is no different to 'slasher' horror movies that fetishise serial killers and rely on gratuitous depictions of violence, often towards young women. Distasteful as it is, it sells DVDs and seats in cinemas. And it also sells records: Cannibal Corpse and Deicide are not small-fry bands playing obscure venues; they play to tens of thousands of people across the world and their members are multi-millionaires.

Nader loved death metal for its ability to shock, for how it dared to say what couldn't be said. As a natural rebel, he was drawn to it. Nader wanted his exhibition, *Faceless*, to be put to music, so he made contact with some of the bands he grew up listening to, Emperor, Morbid Angel, Testament and Obituary. Musicians from all four bands contributed on a track for the show, which was later picked up by a second gallery in New York, who wanted a live performance to supplement Nader's art. He gradually put together a loose coalition of musicians from these seminal death metal bands under his own name – Nader Sadek – and in 2011 released his first album, *In the Flesh*.

The music is raucous, industrial death metal with all the hallmarks of the genre: fast, tremolo-picked guitars, deep growled vocals and blast beats. Rather than channelling the gore and horror-obsessed Cannibal Corpse, Nader's lyrics are closer to Deicide's, taking aim at doctrine and ignorance, religion and greed. *In The Flesh* draws on Nader's fascination with the oil industry, and the impact that it has on humanity. In many of the music videos that accompany the songs, desert settings are interspersed with machinery and industry. Oil is seen as a destructive force, responsible for the wars and bloodshed that have racked Nader's native Middle East. In the second track, 'Petrophilia', Nader argues that the world's thirst for oil has turned it from a commodity to a god. In another, 'Of This Flesh', he takes aim at religion: "Desecration of your idols | Annihilate what's blasphemy | Your holy house of God is burning | Reign a new god of infamy."

On 25 January 2011, a pro-democracy protest brought tens of thousands to the streets of Cairo and within three weeks Hosni Mubarak, who had led Egypt for over 30 years, had been forced from power. For weeks, millions of Egyptians had marched in Cairo, Alexandria and across the country. They had braved tear gas and tanks. They had been charged by gangs of armed thugs riding camels and police armed with riot shields and batons. Many had been injured, and many had died. But they had prevailed.

On 11 February 2011, Mubarak stood down and across the world anyone with a heart felt it swell. In those heady days of the revolution, Tahrir Square was like a carnival. Locals set up free cinemas and concerts; there was poetry, music and street art. In New York, Nader watched what happened and decided that, despite his growing profile in the US, it was time to go home. Arriving in Cairo, he found the metal scene a total free-for-all: "There was no leadership. There was a lot you could get away with," he said.

For decades, Mubarak and his cronies had cracked down on freedom of expression. Musicians, poets and writers – Muslim, Christian and atheist alike – had often been exiled or thrown in jail. Live shows generally had been risky and rare; for metal bands they were rarer still. Even walking the streets with long hair and a guitar was dangerous.

It all dated back to 22 January 1997, when Egyptian police dressed in full riot gear and carrying machine guns kicked in doors in upscale neighbourhoods across Cairo. Young men were dragged out of bed and thrown into waiting police vans, where they were roughed up and handcuffed.

A fortnight earlier, at a gig in downtown Cairo, Alexandria band Volcano Spell had been on stage when someone in the crowd held up an inverted cross. In a picture that survives today, a fan in a black vest can be seen raising the huge wooden crucifix and looking directly at the camera. A few in the crowd are laughing, others are filming the event on their mobile phones. A second picture shows only the top of the cross and a group of other metalheads appearing to remonstrate with the man holding it. The picture somehow found its way into the hands of the local police, who attended and secretly filmed a second show a week later.

Whether it was the music, the headbanging, the black clothes and long hair of the fans or the general atmosphere of angry debauchery, the authorities decided to act. Following the raids, the media smelled blood. Just as the newspapers in Europe had covered the antics of the Norwegian black metal scene in the 1990s, so the media leapt on the lurid stories of drugs, devil worship, sex and the occult that emanated from live metal shows in Cairo and Alexandria.

Muhammed Saad, the author of an Arabic book about this period, has reams of newspaper clippings alleging wild parties, seances and sexual impropriety that equally titillated and outraged both Muslims and Christians across Egypt. Even prior to 1997, there had been a backlash against the rock scene, with cartoons appearing in the press depicting metalheads as goats, alluding to the traditional depiction of Satan. As the media attention grew, more and more rumours began circulating about what young men and women were doing at the few metal shows that were held in Egypt.

Muhammed felt that the media was encouraged by state security, which didn't like the fact that young Egyptian men were gathering en masse to listen to loud, angry music. One particularly dangerous headline in *The Egyptian Gazette*, then Egypt's only English-language newspaper, claimed that Mossad had been orchestrating 'satanic orgies' in Egypt. "Israeli girls flirted with two Egyptian young people and persuaded them to jon [sic] their Satanic group," it claimed, according to a 1997 article in the *Los Angeles Times*. It was not the first time that heavy metal had been linked with Israel; in Lebanon it was reported that headbanging derived from the praying of Orthodox Jews at the Western Wall in Jerusalem.

Within days, most of those arrested had been freed for lack of evidence, but the police were still searching for 19 others who had slipped the net. The Egyptian media helpfully informed the public that satanists could be identified by their black nail polish and lipstick. Under interrogation, the young metal fans were asked bizarre questions about what took place at live metal shows, including whether they drank blood. The men who were charged were accused of a variety of offences including, again, devil worshipping, promoting extreme ideas, committing obscene acts and possession of drugs. Some were held for more than three weeks, although none were ever convicted of a crime.

The raids coincided with an international shift in the metal scene, the effects of which were felt in Egypt and across the world. Europe at the beginning of the 1990s had witnessed the 'second wave' of black metal, a sub-genre associated with paganism and devil worship and pioneered by controversial bands like Burzum and Mayhem. Scandinavian bands were involved in high-profile acts of violence and church burnings that brought what was once a niche subculture into the popular view, gaining coverage not just in Norway but across the world.

Extreme metal's association with irreligiousness and satanism was nothing new, of course, but the second wave brought it into the mainstream. It ensured that those not previously aware of black metal would forever associate *all* metal with the occult and with worship of the devil. In Europe and the US in the 1990s, the consequences of this for fans, at least, were a few disapproving glances and occasional efforts by the authorities to shut down shows. In Egypt it led to arrests, violence and persecution that last until this day.

It did not take long before bands began to play again in Cairo. A year after the arrests, Mohammed H, a veteran of the 1990s scene and founder of Cairo band x-Beyond East, attended his first show aboard a huge boat on the Nile. But the musicians were still cautious. The four bands on the bill played cover songs and sang with clean vocals rather than the guttural growl of traditional extreme metal. It was self-censorship, said Mohammed – known as 'Shung'. "Even for the normal clean music they would consider it satanic, so can you imagine what would happen with a brutal voice?"

Shung had been an outsider on the scene at first, being one of very few metalheads who had grown up in Imbaba, a dirt poor and deeply conservative neighbourhood of Cairo. Like elsewhere in the Middle East, most metal fans and musicians were from middle-class families, living in neighbourhoods where it was easier to get CDs and tapes and with parents who were more tolerant of their children's unorthodox tastes. But Shung and his friends could not afford to buy the expensive imported CDs, tapes or magazines such as *Metal Hammer*, so they would either steal them or copy them from friends. He would walk miles across the city with his guitar to play or to attend shows.

He was attracted to metal because, he said, "it was as hard and dramatic as we were". It was also egalitarian: in a city like Cairo, so divided between rich and poor, Shung was never judged on his background. Nobody cared if he was a Muslim or Christian, whether he was rich or poor . He recalled:

> We all respected each other. There were no borders
> between our minds. We dressed in the same black
> stuff. We felt the passion of the music. We talked
> out our feelings, hopes and beliefs. We were metal.
> One culture. One class. It was one of the rare areas
> in the world where we were all the same.

It was this spirit that drew many young Egyptians towards heavy metal. Sameh, a Christian Egyptian, was brought up in Kuwait before moving to Cairo in 2000. He started university as a Christian in a largely Islamic city, an alternative music fan in a conservative country. He recalled being shunned by the rich students because he was not part of the Cairo elite, but also rejected by the poor students because of his expatriate background. Sameh needed a tribe, and in Cairo's tight-knit heavy metal community, he found one. "I was stuck between different groups, none of which accepted me. I was always a minority in my life. I was a minority in Kuwait as an Egyptian. I was a minority in Egypt as a Christian. I was a minority because I listened to heavy metal," Sameh said. But from the first time he arrived on the Egyptian metal scene, he was never treated as an outsider. "Metal's message is that there is one brotherhood."

But if there was one issue that the scene was never able to solve, Sameh admitted, it was that then – as now – it was almost entirely dominated by men. "That was a major problem," he said. "It was a sausage fest."

Sameh had laughed when he used the American term to describe the gender balance on the Egyptian scene, but for the few women involved in heavy metal in the country it was no joke. Cherine Amr, singer and lead guitarist in Egyptian metal band Massive Scar Era, founded her band with an all-girl line-up because her parents would not allow her to share practice space with male musicians. Along with violinist Nancy Mounir, Cherine recruited two friends to play bass and drums and they quickly wrote enough material to hold shows. She hoped that by playing live she could convince her parents that it was perfectly normal for young women to want to form bands. "When we started playing music, girls were not in bands. We had so many girls with their mums and dads coming to my show, and when I'd come off stage they would say to their parents, 'See, she is a decent woman,'" she said.

When Cherine started out, she would give guitar lessons to young women to avoid the risk of them being assaulted or harassed by their private teachers. Not only as a female Egyptian metal singer, but as an Egyptian woman generally, life was a constant struggle. "Women have become so powerful in my generation, and men have been shocked by this. They have discovered that they are not like their mothers. I'm not going to go down and wash your feet. I'm not going to make food for you while you sit watching TV," she said.

Cherine's vocals in Massive Scar Era – also known as Mascara – are both heavy and clean, one minute melodic, the next a growl. Nancy's violin rides above the chugging, distorted riffs and pounding drums. Aside from being Egyptian, Mascara are a very different band, with a sound that draws from both melodic death metal and folk.

But despite their talent, the band faced issues within what was an overwhelmingly male metal scene in Cairo. Like elsewhere in the world, there are few women in hardcore and metal bands – and even where there are, they are vastly outnumbered at shows. "People refused to listen to our music because we were labelled as a girl band. A lot of them heard that we are going on tour and they said it's because we go naked on stage," she said. Cherine said she felt that those in the local scene who criticised Massive Scar Era were jealous of their success. "They knew that we faced a lot. We had spent a lot of time doing our music. But at the same time they didn't want to confirm to themselves that they were not putting in the effort."

By 2005, the scene had largely recovered from the arrests of 1997 and extreme bands such as Mascara were writing their own music, instead of playing covers. Muhammed Saad helped launch a website, EgyptMetal. net, which brought together not only bands from Cairo and

Alexandria but from Jordan, Syria and Lebanon, including Beirut's Kaoteon and Jordan's Bilocate. They used the site not only to share music and publicise shows but to learn lessons from other bands about how to avoid falling foul of the authorities.

Using these connections, they brought both Bilocate and Nervecell, a Dubai-based death metal band, to Cairo. The momentum grew and by the mid-2000s Egypt was experiencing its own 'second wave' of metal. Two of the bands to emerge were Dark Philosophy, who are one of very few black metal bands in Cairo, and Scarab, probably Egypt's most famous death metal band, who formed from the remnants of Hate Suffocation. But Egyptian metal fans and musicians were not totally spared the hysteria of the 1990s nor the damaging association with satanism. In 2005, a local newspaper named Muhammed Saad, Sameh Sabry and Dark Philosophy's singer Noor Hamed as the organisers of a "Satanic cell" after they organised a gig in Cairo.

The day the story came out, Sameh remembered having to go to speak to his father: "My father laughed. He said this was a cheap newspaper anyway, and that there was no such thing as bad publicity." But there was a serious side: although Muhammed, Noor and Sameh were not arrested or interrogated, being named by a popular newspaper as satanists was dangerous at a time when radical Islamist groups were active in Egypt. As well as naming the three men, the newspaper had revealed where Sameh was study-ing. "If you put this paper in front of a group of extremists, any one of them might want to kill me and go to heaven," he said.

Islamist vigilantes never acted, but there were still constant issues with the police. Often shows would be closed for permit violations and, as a result, Egyptian promoters had to choose venues further and further away from the city. "Life was hard," said Sameh. "People were threatening us – I think I got used to being threatened. Every concert we attended or every concert we arranged we were always expecting that the police would shut it down. Or the organiser would be arrested. Or there would be an article in the newspaper speaking about us."

It is largely because of the arrests in 1997 that the wider world found out about the Egyptian metal scene, but Muhammed said that there is a tendency today to over-glamorise the 1990s:

> Let's be fair, the Egyptian scene at that time wasn't that good. There was no gear, no guitar tabs, no lyrics, no T-shirts – nothing. The bands used to sing the songs without knowing the lyrics. You watch footage of the old shows and you can easily count the number of metal T-shirts you can see.

He contrasts that with the early to mid-2000s, when, despite the problems with the police, there were at least three major metal events every summer. Even huge branded festivals sponsored by companies such as Vodafone were allowing one metal band to perform on the bill, and when the media left metalheads alone, the police tended to follow suit.

> As much as our authorities sound aggressive to the media, they would rather not make problems for no reason. If you are playing music in your house and nobody complains, a police officer won't arrest you. But if you make a problem, they might have to. In my opinion the media was directing this idea that people were praising Satan, drinking blood and having group sex – you have attended a lot of concerts: did you ever see anybody drinking blood?

Occasional raids took place, and in 2009 there was a bizarre countrywide crackdown on Egypt's growing 'emo' scene that saw dozens of young, eyeliner-wearing men rounded up as homosexuals.

But the rise of bands like Mascara, Scarab and Dark Philosophy in Egypt's second wave during the mid-2000s came alongside the growth of something else in Egypt: vocal calls for political reform. Hosni Mubarak had come to power in 1980 with a promise that he would not be the traditional president-for-life strongman and would instead introduce economic and political reform. For 25 years, Egyptians had watched Mubarak and his cronies steadily sell off the country's assets and increase their vice-like grip over the social and political realm. Their anger would build into a movement that would capture the world and change the country and the music scene forever. Within a few years, Muhammed, Shung, Cherine and Sameh, like millions of other Egyptians, would find their lives turned upside down.

* * *

On 30 January 2011, 23-year-old Ramy Essam was at home in Mansoura when the city's police abandoned their positions. In Cairo, hundreds of thousands had already gathered in Tahrir Square, transforming a once traffic-clogged intersection into a symbol of freedom and resistance for millions throughout Egypt, the wider Middle East, and the world. Protesters in Cairo had marched, chanted and sung, and Egyptians across the country had started doing the same. Now, in Mansoura, just down the Nile, the police had stood down. The protesters could hardly believe it – the streets were theirs.

Like many young Egyptians, Ramy had grown up listening to western bands like Nirvana and Rage Against the Machine. He grew his hair long and began composing his own songs on a guitar given to him by his elder brother,

Shadi, who had raised him since his father died when he was 11. But despite his love of politically tinged metal and grunge, Ramy's own compositions were mostly love songs. He was young, living in a small city, and there wasn't much chance to play heavy metal. He told his teachers he wanted to be an architect, but his real dream was to be a musician.

Like a generation of young people in Egypt, it was protest that politicised Ramy. He remembered how, despite the absence of authority, there was no chaos, looting or violence. Ordinary Egyptians protected not just what they had but their friends and neighbours. "When I saw that, my faith grew stronger and stronger. Everything I saw made me love the revolution," he said.

Like the tens of thousands of Egyptians across the country, he packed his bags for Cairo to join the crowds, not forgetting his guitar.

Ramy found Tahrir pulsing with people and a stage already erected for regular speeches and music by Cairo-based bands. He hovered nervously around the tents that had been erected in the centre of the square and began listening to the protesters' chants, improvising a few chords and finding melodies. As his sketches coalesced into songs, his music spread. At some point, someone urged him to get up on the stage. But, as a 23-year-old with a ponytail and a guitar, he wasn't sure how the crowds would react. A steward, standing on the steps up to the stage, blocked his path. "Don't worry," Ramy said to him, "I'm not here to play love songs – you're going to like this." He agreed to give him five minutes. Ramy plugged in his guitar, and looked out at the hundreds of thousands of men and women standing before him. He began to play.

The songs that the protesters sung in Cairo before Ramy arrived had their origins in the music of two giants of Egypt: Ahmed Fouad Negm and Sheikh Imam. Born in an impoverished village in Egypt's Nile Delta in 1929, Negm composed his poetry in the gritty slang of the Egyptian street and was a thorn in the side of every Egyptian leader from Gamal Abdel Nasser to Mubarak. He met Sheikh Imam, a blind oud player and together they threw themselves into the student-led protests against the Nasser regime.

Negm found his voice as a poet during his and Sheikh Imam's regular bouts of incarceration. He sympathised with his fellow prisoners, many of whom had been jailed for years for political offences. In 2011, decades after they had been composed, the crowds in Tahrir chanted Negm and Sheikh Imam's songs in opposition to another Egyptian dictator, Mubarak. The Sheikh did not live to see the moment (he died in 1995) but Negm was received with a hero's welcome in Tahrir.

A day before Mubarak stood down, Negm was on stage with Ramy, who by now was being hailed as 'the voice of Tahrir'. Using chants inspired by Negm's poems, and putting them to music, Ramy had crystallised generations of opposition to Egyptian autocracy. A few weeks later, after Mubarak had stood down, Negm and Ramy met again by chance at a cafe in downtown Cairo. Negm told Ramy that he had heard of his reputation as the voice of Tahrir and asked him to play. When he finished, he said only three words: "you deserve it". "I have never forgotten that," Ramy said.

Ramy composed the song that was to make him famous in a tent in Tahrir Square. Mubarak had just made his second speech to the nation, suggesting that he would never stand down, and protesters had started to get calls from their families asking them to come home. Ramy composed a simple message to the once mighty dictator of Egypt: 'Irhal' ('Leave'). The lyrics fused the chants that protesters were using in the square with a catchy and simple song in a folky, flamenco style. His performance of 'Irhal' in Tahrir went viral after it was posted on YouTube. Within five years, Ramy's song had been ranked alongside John Lennon's 'Imagine' and Public Enemy's 'Fight the Power' in *Time Out* magazine's '100 Songs that Changed History'. The song turned the public mood after Mubarak's speech. "It was a special moment, at 23 years old, standing on the stage with 200,000 people singing along with me," he said.

Cairo's metalheads were also swept up in the revolution. Muhammed Saad spent days and weeks in Tahrir and still has a picture taken in 2011 of him, Sameh and half a dozen other

Egyptian musicians waving a Slayer flag in the square during the last days of Mubarak. Overnight, a deeply entrenched and oppressive police state disappeared and the metal scene could suddenly organise shows with impunity. Noor Hamed, the lead singer of Dark Philosophy, played music so extreme that the band struggled to play in Cairo prior to the revolution. But after 25 January, all of that changed. "Before January 25th you couldn't find any extreme black or death metal bands in Egypt. We played concerts in private homes of my friends, not in public places. But after, you could find extreme metal everywhere – you could make concerts anywhere," he said.

When the Muslim Brotherhood won Egypt's first democratic elections in 2011 and 2012, there were fears that they would roll back the freedoms from which metallers had benefited in Cairo since the revolution. But, for musicians, Muslim Brotherhood-ruled Egypt was actually freer than Mubarak's. New venues opened and bands began making plans to release albums. The El Sawy Culture Wheel, a hulking concrete edifice on the banks of the River Nile in Zamalek began hosting heavy metal shows again. Owned by Mohammed el-Sawy, minister of culture, it was able to resist efforts on the part of hardliners to clamp down on extreme music.

In 2012, the scene even managed to weather a 'satanism' storm whipped up by an overzealous member of the

Brotherhood, who told a newspaper that metal fans in Cairo were worshipping Satan and disparaging Islam. There were fears that the scandal would mark the end of the era of relative freedom for extreme bands, but then something amazing happened: nobody jumped on the bandwagon. "Most people, when they heard this crazy guy, just said: 'No, that's wrong,'" Noor said. "That was the first time I felt that people were with us. Even the media, who usually call us satanists, this time said: 'No, they are musicians.'" Despite the media long hating Egypt's metallers, it seemed they hated the Brotherhood more.

Not that conservatism wasn't still a problem. El Sawy was still the only venue in Cairo to host bands as heavy as Dark Philosophy and Noor regularly had to tell the crowd not to mosh, while drinking and smoking were both forbidden. "It was still easier than before January 25, but it wasn't as easy as right after the revolution. We had more rules. It was suffocating," Noor said. But at the same time he felt that, at last, Egyptian society was beginning to stop seeing heavy metal as a threat. "Yes, there were people who questioned us, but more people understood metal. Some people said we were not normal, but I said don't clash with them. If we were normal with them, it would make metal easier to understand."

For Cherine, the challenges remained. At El Sawy, she not only had to run her lyrics past the organisers to check she wasn't saying anything too contentious, but a female member of staff would approve her and Nancy's outfits before they went on stage. But life was easier than it had been under Mubarak: "I didn't feel that I was that constrained while the Brotherhood was there. I actually felt that we had more freedom then. Which is weird. I did not see that coming," she said.

There are a lot of theories as to why the Muslim Brotherhood never instigated the same kind of crackdown on heavy metal that the Mubarak-era authorities had done. Cherine's theory isn't that the Muslim Brotherhood were particularly tolerant of musicians, rather that they had bigger problems to deal with. They probably would have wanted to crack down on heavy metal, they just didn't have the resources to do so.

As the protests in Cairo raged, hundreds gathered outside President Mohammed Morsi's palace every night and demonstrators fought pitched battles on the streets with the police and armed forces. There was still a stage in Tahrir, and Ramy Essam was still on it, but he had changed the lyrics to his song 'Irhal'. Now, the person he wanted to leave was Morsi.

* * *

On 30 June 2013, tanks rolled down the streets of Cairo and a military coup marked the end of the Egyptian army's tolerance with Morsi and the revolution. Like most Egyptians in Cairo, Ramy Essam was glad that Morsi had been ousted – but he was never going to support military rule in his place. He found that opinion less and less well received in Tahrir. He recalled:

> The square was full of supporters from the army and I couldn't accept it. I went to the stage and I started to sing against the military. In the square there were usually hundreds of thousands of people singing along: but it didn't happen. I told them we should never forget what the military did to us. How they killed and tortured people. We should not support them. But some people jeered. They didn't understand.

Ramy regrets that the revolution didn't persevere. "We should have continued pushing from that day," he said, referring to 11 February, when Mubarak stood down. "We left: that was the most stupid thing. They succeeded in pushing the media and everyone to make it a personal fight between the people and Mubarak – everything became about him as a person and not as the regime."

Ramy's views following the coup of 30 June and the installation of General Sisi as Egypt's new leader were not popular, and he found gigs less and less easy to find.

He began playing at private parties and then even those invitations dried up. "I couldn't play again after Sisi came. It was crazy. It was like someone turned a key. I was so big and strong and playing everywhere in the revolution and real concerts and then it was like someone said, 'No, Ramy'. My music was forbidden from the radio; it still is now." He wondered what he had done to warrant being snubbed by people he had considered his friends. Things got so bad that Ramy moved back to Mansoura with his parents, his new wife, Mai, and his newborn son.

> I didn't have any income to live, to eat. I was so poor.
> I was happy to be home, but it wasn't a nice time
> in my life. I wanted to understand what happened:
> because I was this totally unknown guy and then in
> a few days I became huge. I stayed like that for two-
> and-a-half years and then suddenly I lost it all.

In the end, Ramy realised that people were tired of fighting and when they heard his songs they just wanted to switch off. He decided he would have to accept losing fans to stay true to his beliefs and message. But there was a more pressing matter at play. He would soon be 28, meaning that he would have to do his compulsory military service. Given Ramy's years of outspoken criticism towards the military, he and his family feared for his safety – even his life – if he had to join up. He had received threats via social media by serving soldiers. Even without the threats, he could not stomach the idea of serving in an army that had beaten, tortured and murdered Egyptians on the streets of Cairo. In August 2014 he was able to get permission to leave the country, and flew to Sweden with his wife and son.

Cherine also felt more and more like a stranger in Egypt and was frustrated that others did not feel the same. She found herself getting annoyed not just at the big things, but by the little ones too: "You know I was the only one in my building complaining about people throwing garbage in front of my door. The mindset is just different and it seems like everyone is just going along with it. So I might as well leave, go somewhere I can fit," she said.

In 2015 she emigrated to Canada, and the country has given her that. Even if her songs still deal with issues that relate to Egypt, it has allowed her to take a step back from Cairo. But she finds that Canadians cannot get their head around the fact that Cherine is a practising Muslim and sings in a heavy metal band. "The usual stereotype is different so they are seeing another side of Islam too, which can get interesting, especially in the lyrics," she said.

Cherine receives messages from fans in Egypt – often young women – who talk about how inspired they are by her songs, but she does not feel like she has to move back to Egypt to be part of changing the mindset in that country: "I have done my best. I am 30 now; I started this when I was 19 and I don't want to live my youth just fighting for something that I know people don't want." Equally, Cherine does not believe that music can achieve change in Egypt. "The majority of Egyptians are poor and illiterate – more than 50 per cent are below the poverty line. I don't think that these people would want to listen to a song rather than find food for their children. I don't know how to fix that," she said.

The government recently gave the hated state-sponsored musicians' syndicate the power of arrest as a result, the very organisation that should be protecting musicians was instead persecuting them. "It is a disaster: you could perform in a concert and you could find yourself being arrested. We know a lot of people who are in jail," she said.

As for Muhammed and Noor, they remain in Cairo as metal fans and continue to get by. For Noor, the new generation of bands lacks the soul of the old one, and the regular satanism scares have made playing all but impossible. Sisi may have overthrown the Muslim Brotherhood, but he has made much of his status as a pious Muslim leader, and an increasing number of writers, poets and artists have been jailed on charges of blasphemy since he took office. The rumours of satanism, sex and subversion that destroyed Egypt's metal scene in the 1990s have returned, and if the arrest of Nader and the shutting down of the Sepultura show in 2016 were warnings, they were effective ones.

A celebrated novelist, a well-known cartoonist and even a serving soldier who posted a mocked-up picture of Sisi with Mickey Mouse ears (not to mention thousands of political prisoners and activists) were all jailed during 2016 by the Egyptian regime. Given that, most Egyptian metalheads figure that now is not the time to be pushing for more creative freedom. As it stands, El Sawy remains the only venue that hosts heavy metal gigs and regular rows between various promoters of concerts in Cairo and Alexandria mean that the scene is divided. Noor's fight has gone: "We have no power to do anything new. Our old guitarist is not in Egypt now. Our drummer is married. I have two children," he said. "I have to work hard to make money. You can't do music and fight for this – you can only fight to eat."

For Muhammed, it doesn't seem so long ago that he and his friends headed to Tahrir during the revolution and raised a Slayer flag. Now, with the shutting down of the Sepultura show, there is a fear that the bad old days might soon return. "It has become difficult, because no one can stand against the state. If national security think that a metal concert will disturb the peace of society then they will shut you down," he said. He feels beaten; he feels old:

I am still living in the past, when we used to trade metal tapes and explore new metal music. I still remember the preparation that I had to make to go to a metal concert, the orgasm that happens when you hear metal music live from local bands, the mosh pits and the headbanging. The pride you feel to own rare metal tapes and to wear a T-shirt for a band you love.

As for Sameh, he too is nostalgic – for both the revolution and happier times in Egypt's music scene. Sameh has always claimed not to be political, but he threw himself into the revolution in 2011 alongside Muhammed and the rest of the metal scene. He remembers the two of them going down to Tahrir Square when it was still occupied and, donning rubber gloves, joining the rest of the square in scrubbing and cleaning the protest space that had given birth to the revolution.

But he still thinks that Egypt was fundamentally changed by what happened in February 2011. "Before the revolution, people were not speaking about problems. They were afraid to speak, in general. But after that, people became less afraid to share their opinions," he said. Egyptian metalheads always felt shunned by Egypt, they felt like outsiders in their own country, but the revolution brought them back home. When they stood in Tahrir Square, they were finally part of Egypt's future. "Before the revolution we listened to the music and we hoped. After the revolution we listened to the music, we hoped – and we acted," he said. Sameh has since moved to Dubai for work, but has only fond memories of the tribe:

> We had this vibe. We had this fire. We had these feelings. Man, you used to get a tape that was completely fucked up and you could barely listen to the sound and you could barely listen to the music and your brother might have recorded something over the middle of the song and you still enjoyed every second of it.

Sameh's business and life in the UAE now keep him too busy to be involved in the metal scene. He is married and the vice president of a global IT company. His new life has made him paranoid about taking part in the Egyptian scene as he once did, and on his last trip to Cairo he did not attend a show. "Fifteen years ago I was a nameless teenager. Right now I am vice president for a big company. I have a family. It's not worth it. To get into a big problem for listening to music in a place," he said.

But still today, when he is interviewed in the media about his work, he always drops in the fact that he is a metal fan:

> They portray us as losers and drug addicts and useless people – so I had a different motive. When

I grew up I wanted to be successful to promote heavy metal as a positive resource rather than a destructive one. I used to make it clear in TV interviews and newspaper interviews that I listened to heavy metal. People would say: "Oh, you are wearing a full suit and an expensive tie and you look like those guys. How come you listen to heavy metal?" And I'd say: "What does me wearing a suit have anything to do with it?"

It still frustrates him, from afar, that the concept of a successful, normal heavy metal fan is not one that the media globally – let alone in Egypt – is interested in. While the crackdowns over the past 20 years on Egyptian metal are for the most part spurious, sensational nonsense, there are those on the metal scene in Cairo and elsewhere who play up to the rumours.

He remembers hosting a gig years ago and overhearing a young metal fan saying she wanted to sacrifice a cat to Satan. He told her to leave. "I said it is because of people like you that we are being insulted. When Egyptian media wanted to invite heavy metal fans on TV they invited those that would sell: with 10,000 piercings and long hair and tattoos. They didn't interview me. They didn't invite other successful people. Why? Because it doesn't sell."

* * *

By 2015, Nader had arranged three successful shows – including one by Belgian death metal veterans Aborted. But in 2016 his fourth, by German black metal band Dark Fortress, was cancelled. His success in bringing international acts to Egypt was resented by some of the promoters on the Cairo scene, as it was by some of the local bands. But Nader held in open contempt many of the bands that had tolerated the repression of the Mubarak era by taking money from the government or playing state-sanctioned shows. "The shit that is, for the lack of a better word, controversial – those are the bands that I respect. The ones that are playing it safe and getting government money and sucking up to authorities – that is the exact opposite."

Nader has been inspired by early death and black metal bands in the US and Europe – as well as by Lebanon's Ayat – and the challenges they had playing extreme metal in similarly difficult settings. He believes Middle East bands should be following that lead. "When Deicide and Cannibal Corpse were doing this shit, it wasn't accepted – some of those guys got arrested and attacked by politicians. If you're going to do this, you have a responsibility, you know what I mean?"

It is that responsibility, Nader said, that brought him back to Egypt – despite the fact that he has a successful career in the US. Even after his arrest in 2016, he was back in Cairo planning more shows. "Egypt has got to change, man," he said.

* * *

With his new life in Sweden, Ramy is many thousands of miles from Cairo. Many years from the magic of Tahrir. But he still writes songs about Egypt. His heart is still there. And he still plans to return. He has been convinced that however bad it is in Egypt, it can be better.

When others say that the revolution failed, that Egypt cannot be saved, Ramy looks to the youth, to his fans. Every day he wakes up to messages from Egyptian teenagers who have heard his music and who want to fight for their freedom, to fight corruption, to go back to the end of the 11 days in 2011 and take a different path. "They are still so young and so pure and not fucked up by life. They understand my lyrics. They are discussing the songs with me. They are saying stuff that I only started to think about when I was 21," he said.

Ramy's generation looked to newspapers and television for their news, they were brainwashed by state-owned media. But the internet has changed all that. "We watched TV and listened to radio and read newspapers and were fucked up but we have a new generation that is really thirsty to learn. The Egyptian government can't control social media. It is over," he said. "These guys are really free, free to choose their path."

CHAPTER 4
SAUDI ARABIA

A harsh desert sun beat down as two cars full of young men wearing black Gorerotted, Rotten Sound and Doom T-shirts approached the remote, sand-swept border that Saudi Arabia shares with the United Arab Emirates. Beneath the concrete arches, a green sign proclaimed "Welcome to Saudi Arabia" as mile upon mile of arid, flat, grubby desert stretched to the horizon on both sides.

Up ahead, Saudi officials were ordering passengers out of their cars to search for illicit materials: drugs, alcohol or pornography. As the two cars edged forward in the queue that snaked back along the road, the eyes of the border guards widened. They had spent all day checking great hulking freight lorries and the odd family SUV returning from a shopping trip to Dubai, and suddenly a dozen young men with beards and shaved heads arrive with guitars on their laps and wearing black T-shirts and jeans. This was probably the most interesting thing to happen at this remote border outpost all year.

They ordered the men out of the cars and took two of them, Fawaz and Talal, away for questioning. The guards dived inside the vehicles and started pulling out CDs, instruments and a huge black banner with a scrawled white logo on a black background. In the boot of one of the cars they found a box of T-shirts all carrying the same logo, white on black in a semi-legible scrawl: *Creative Waste*.

Chris Leamy, an American teacher living in Riyadh, was travelling back to Saudi Arabia with the band that day and remembered the young men politely arguing over the 't' in the Creative Waste logo, which the border officials said looked like a Christian cross. This was a serious allegation in a strictly Muslim country where other strains of Islam are barely tolerated, let alone Christianity. "They were close to going to jail for it," Leamy said. It took two hours for Fawaz and Talal to persuade the police that the T-shirts were related to horror movies – not religion – but the officials still confiscated all their merchandise and the banner.

Despite the loss, the band felt lucky. They had planned to pick up a box of CDs in Dubai – copies of their new album, *Slaves of Conformity*, which had been shipped from India. In the end, the shipping had been delayed. If the Saudi authorities had discovered the CDs – which included the lyrics to songs critical of Saudi Arabia and its rulers – they would almost certainly have been arrested. In fact, it had been a relief that the officials had suspected the guys of being a gaggle of proselytising Christians – something that they certainly were not – rather than a grindcore band, which they absolutely were.

It was a rough end to what had otherwise been a great weekend. Creative Waste were on the bill with US death metal veterans Hate Eternal, and even those within the metal community in Dubai had been shocked that the authorities had permitted such an extreme group to play.

Dubai and Abu Dhabi had hosted a handful of rock shows in 2012, including Guns N' Roses and Metallica, and the UAE was rapidly emerging as a hub for metal bands from across the region. As the Arab Spring raged, Dubai was attracting tens of thousands of middle-class Arabs who wanted to sit out the political turmoil and had taken jobs in the emirate. It was also relatively liberal, and home to millions of expatriates from across the Arab world, the Indian subcontinent and the West. The government had realised that, just like high-profile sporting events like Formula One, big name shows at venues such as Yas Island, near Abu Dhabi, brought in both money and cachet.

But Hate Eternal were different. A relatively unknown act outside a close-knit international death metal scene, their music was fast, uncompromising and brutal, with lyrics that, although largely unintelligible (in keeping with the style of the genre), deal with religion, violence and misanthropy. Metallica hadn't been *that* kind of band in over 20 years. In all likelihood, Hate Eternal had only got to play in Dubai because the promoter had operated under the radar. The venue – a grotty Irish pub in a two-star hotel in the suburbs – was far from being an arena. In a city so well known for glitzy malls, celebrity guests and tall towers, it was the closest Dubai had to a dive bar.

But for bands from Saudi Arabia, even Dubai's dives were a lifeline. There had been discreet scenes in Jeddah, on the Red Sea coast, and al-Khobar and Dammam, in the east, for over two decades, but playing live in the country had been all but impossible for at least three years prior to Creative Waste's show with Hate Eternal. King Abdullah bin Abdulaziz, who took power in 2005, was known as a reformer who wanted to see more women in school and more Saudis travelling overseas to study in the US or Europe. But this was Saudi Arabia: like his brothers who had ruled before him, King Abdullah had to deal with the fact that, outside the main cities, millions of Saudis did not want to see women in the streets, let alone in universities.

Since the 1980s, Saudi clerics had branded music *haram*, or forbidden. The rest of the Arab world was free to laugh at ridiculous rulings by these bearded old men but Saudis were not: religious law was enforced by the club-wielding fanatics of the Committee for the Promotion of Virtue and the Prevention of Vice, who would prowl the streets looking for all signs of immodesty or dissent. While King Abdullah was trying to modernise the economy, the Wahhabi religious clerics who held such immense power in Saudi Arabia were busy banning snowmen, emojis and Pokémon.

Of all the world's ugly police states, Saudi Arabia is the one least likely to sustain a metal scene. Not only are all three of the proverbial 'sex, drugs and rock 'n' roll' heavily curtailed, if not illegal, but the country has been branded a "veritable wasteland for human rights" by Human Rights Watch. Even if Saudi heavy metal bands are not anti-religious or anti-state – and most are not – the imagery of the genre is enough to cause serious problems for the young men (and it is almost entirely young men) who play in bands in the kingdom. The last live show to be held in Saudi Arabia in 2009 resulted in the arrest, jailing and deportation of the organisers. Before that night, there hadn't been a show since 2006.

As in other Middle East countries, only a tiny handful of bands across the region are anti-religious, let alone devil worshipping, but that doesn't matter: those 'satanist' slurs that have been tossed around in Lebanon and Egypt are far more serious in Saudi Arabia. In 2012, blogger Raif Badawi was sentenced to 600 lashes for calling for democratic reform. Hamza Kashgari, a 23-year-old poet, was jailed for two years for making comments on a blog that were deemed an insult to the Prophet Mohammed.

"Hear our screams of torment / We were born into bondage / Left to wander / Living in the shadow of their light," Fawaz screams in Creative Waste's song 'Low Born'. Behind his deep growl, the guitar riffs are angular and atonal, and Talal's drums pound away in a frantic counterpoint. This is grindcore, and it comes from a dark place. Fawaz, Talal and Essam, Creative Waste's guitarist, are not stereotypical Saudis with fast cars and flowing robes. Qatif, their home town, is not Riyadh, with its tall towers and its mega-malls. Creative Waste are members of Saudi Arabia's Shia minority, and the Shia in Saudi are the low born, a three-million-strong minority in a country where Sunni Wahhabi fanatics see them as apostates and heretics.

In 2012, when they drove to Dubai to play with Hate Eternal, Qatif was the volatile heart of a protest movement that channelled the Arab Spring and brought thousands of angry Shia to the streets to call for rights and democracy. But their struggle was met in the same way the Saudi state has always dealt with dissent: with violence.

Before the show, Creative Waste holed up in a Mexican-themed bar in the bustling district of Bur Dubai, taking up two long tables in the centre of the restaurant, throwing back margaritas and beers. Earlier that day they had all been to Dubai's huge water park, Wild Wadi, and then to see a movie at the cinema. Booze, movies and water parks: a day out they could never have in Saudi Arabia.

At the venue, a run-down Irish bar in the back of a Holiday Inn, the band colonised a few tables to the right of the stage. The room began to fill with young men in black T-shirts as well as with a handful of female fans, a source of much excitement for the younger members of Creative

Waste's entourage – in Saudi Arabia mixing of the sexes in public is forbidden. Chris Leamy was impressed by the calibre of the metal T-shirts on display: Nunslaughter, Carcass, Witchery, Darkthrone, Ripping Corpse. He had expected a few tired Metallica and Iron Maiden tops but these obscure bands signified that many of the crowd were real connoisseurs of extreme metal.

Most of the crowd had turned out to see Hate Eternal. Despite the fact that Creative Waste had already toured the US as a band, they were still relatively unknown in the Middle East. As such, they were first on the bill. When the time came, Fawaz climbed onto the stage as Essam and Talal started arranging their gear, moving amps and setting up the drum kit. They were playing without a bassist (although Fawaz plays bass on Creative Waste's two albums) and Fawaz stalked up and down the stage, staring at the floor. When the music kicked in, he came alive, pacing back and forth, possessed, growling the vocals over the frantic counterpoint of fast-picked riffs and blast beats: the anarchic timbre of furious grindcore. Those gathered by the bar and around the periphery suddenly stopped talking and turned towards the stage. Creative Waste's entourage were headbanging furiously, throwing each other back and forth in a sea of long hair, arms and elbows as Fawaz screamed and roared over the distortion. Creative Waste are no local pub band – they are polished, tight and disciplined. They play like a single unit led by Fawaz, his eyes focused on the crowd as he paces faster and faster across the stage. Fawaz is fond of saying that his music "rapes your ears", and while he is often laughing when he says it, their music is no joke.

It has often come as a surprise that three young Arabs would get into heavy metal in some forgotten corner of Saudi Arabia – and that, of all the genres out there, they would pick the dirtiest, most chaotic and most anarchic: grind. But just as Napalm Death – the founders of the grindcore genre – arose out of the malaise and frustration of Britain in 1981, so Creative Waste have taken the frustration of life in a violent corner of Saudi Arabia and turned it into furious, uncompromising music. The crowd in Dubai were captivated.

Fawaz was in the eighth grade at the Saudi-run Islamic Saudi Academy in Alexandria, Virginia, when he first met Essam. During class, the pair spoke about music, discovering their shared love of US nu-metal band Korn and of video games like Spawn and Mortal Kombat. As the weeks went by, they decided to start a band and, lacking a drummer, drafted in Fawaz's younger brother, Talal. Fawaz and Talal had grown up listening to Korn, buying their album *Issues* in 1999. None of the three teenagers were able to play an instrument, so they spent their time talking about music.

After Fawaz and Talal finished their schooling in Virginia they headed back to Qatif, with Essam – who had by now acquired a guitar – following a year later. One afternoon he showed up at Fawaz and Talal's house with his two brothers, and sat down to show them his skills. "He played with his guitar upside down and only played one string – most of the others were missing anyway," Fawaz remembered. "We were all sitting in a circle and he was playing random things. I remember him playing Missy Elliott." But despite Essam's basic skills, Fawaz was upbeat: "We all thought: 'Man, this is really going to happen.'"

Creative Waste were born as the internet was just beginning to become accessible in Saudi Arabia, opening their minds to the world of metal beyond Korn and the few other CDs and tapes they had begged, borrowed or stolen from friends. For Fawaz, it began with Canadian technical band Cryptopsy and seminal US death metal band Cannibal Corpse, who are known as much for their pioneering role in the American scene as for their outrageous and offensive lyrics, inspired by an obsession with horror movies.

Cannibal Corpse are one of a few American bands that have been singled out by conservative politicians in the United States, who in the mid-1990s tried to persuade major labels to drop their music. They have been banned in Australia, Canada, Russia and Germany at various periods over the past 20 years. It was this shocking, brutal music that appealed to the three young men from eastern Saudi Arabia. From there, Fawaz discovered Pig Destroyer, a band founded from the ashes of arguably the most controversial grindcore band of all time, Anal Cunt.

Finally, the road through extreme music landed Fawaz, Essam and Talal at the door of one of the most important bands of the grindcore genre, Nasum. Founded in 1992 in Örebro, Sweden, Nasum were grindcore purists whose mission was to bring the genre back to its roots. It was this uncompromising attitude that was to serve as inspiration for Creative Waste. "We just had no idea this type of speed and anger existed," said Fawaz. "It felt right. I think it was what we had been striving for since the beginning."

They met in Fawaz's bedroom in Qatif and Essam would regularly stay over so they could practise throughout the night. Gradually, they accumulated the basic equipment they needed: a small combo amplifier, two guitars and a basic drum kit. For vocals, Fawaz plugged a microphone into a stereo his parents used to play records. That bedroom remains Creative Waste's HQ to this day: "God knows how many hours we've spent in that room," Fawaz said.

Even in the late 1990s and early 2000s, there were a few established metal bands in Saudi Arabia, but Creative Waste knew little about any of them. The internet had already allowed bands from Saudi Arabia's three main hubs – the Eastern Province, Riyadh and Jeddah – to find each other, but there was still no central point for the Saudi metal scene to coalesce around. And Creative Waste were too caught up in writing to spend time searching for other bands. "We mainly lived in my bedroom – we weren't even aware of other musicians until a few years after," he said. "We thought we were the only ones."

* * *

On the west coast of the Arabian Peninsula, Jeddah is as far away from Qatif as it is possible to go without ending up in the Red Sea. It is a sprawling and chaotic city that for centuries has been a thriving port and gateway to the Muslim holy site of Mecca, where Muslims are obliged to make pilgrimage at least once in their lives. Over the centuries, many of those who fulfilled that obligation spent their life savings trekking from the farthest reaches of the Muslim world, but then couldn't afford to get home. Many of them settled in the narrow streets of the old city, *al-balad*, making Jeddah a multicultural city at a time when much of the Arabian Gulf was a backwater.

Maybe because of this mishmash of cultures, Jeddah is not like the rest of Saudi Arabia. When you fly into the city from Dubai, hundreds of miles of rolling dunes finally give way to rugged mountains and then the crystal blue waters of the Red Sea. On the outskirts of the city, vast palaces with fountains and golden domes sit behind concrete walls and fortified guardhouses. Yet Jeddah is far from picturesque: it is overcrowded, disorganised and neglected. Downtown, trash litters the streets and many of the older buildings have been left crumbling into the narrow alleys. Downtown Jeddah often looks more like Gaza than it does the second city of a wealthy Gulf petro-state. This is one of Saudi Arabia's great dichotomies. And it is not the only one.

Ever since the Saudi regime and its zealot backers, the Wahhabis, took control of Jeddah, they have tried to whip and cajole what was once a renowned centre of art, music and literature into line. For the most part, they have succeeded. Live music is mostly banned. Cinemas are banned. Mixing of the sexes, women driving and alcohol are all forbidden. But for Saudis there is still the feeling that Jeddah is different. It may not be possible for a woman to drive a car, but the city is home to the only university in the country that allows both sexes to study together. It may not be possible to organise a live heavy metal show, but it is easy to walk into a music shop and buy a Gibson guitar and a Marshall stack, take them home and start jamming with like-minded friends.

When CNN visited Saudi Arabia in 2010 to meet death metal band Wasted Land, they met them in Jeddah. When, later that year MTV, released their controversial documentary *True Life – Resist the Power, Saudi Arabia*, it was filmed in Jeddah. The city is so used to foreigners, in fact, that its ring road has a special lane for 'Christians' that takes them on a circuitous route to avoid the holy city of Mecca (where it is forbidden for non-Muslims to go). Tell any Saudi that you have an idea what their country is like after visiting Jeddah and they will shake their head and say: "Ah, but Jeddah is different."

Ahmed is a Jeddah native and the frontman in one of Saudi Arabia's only doom metal bands, Grieving Age. The band has released two albums since 2010, the first of which was mastered by Katatonia's Dan Swanö and attracted praise in the international music press. Despite that, in ten years as a band, Grieving Age have performed only once, in Cairo.

Ahmed's day job is as a music distributor, importing foreign CDs ranging from Metallica to Justin Timberlake to be sold in Saudi Arabia's few record stores. One of his main clients was Virgin Megastore in Jeddah, which boasts an impressive heavy metal section. Ahmed knew the shelves in the Virgin outlet deep in the suburbs of Jeddah very well: he had fought Saudi Arabia's censors to bring every one of the CDs into the country. Often the battle would be over cover artwork – particularly on metal albums – but song and band names (as well as lyrics, if they were printed in cover booklets) could also raise eyebrows.

As a genre, doom is slow and heavy with a groove that is lacking in the more extreme styles of death and black metal. Black Sabbath are said to be the forefathers of doom, giving it both its sludgy guitar sound and its huge riffs, but over the past three decades the scene has taken on influences from other genres, from gothic metal to classical music. As they would in a classical symphony, themes rise and fall, drop out and then return, and songs can stretch from eight minutes to over an hour. As for the fans, doomheads are considered to be thinkers, laid-back and thoughtful, liable to mock the excitable fury of grind or death metal and the self-aggrandising misanthropy of black metal.

Alongside death metal, doom is arguably the most popular genre in the Middle East. One reason for this is that, just like in the West, it is accessible. Take a non-metalhead friend to a Napalm Death show and, unless they have a pretty hardy constitution, the discordant riffs, barked vocals and beer-throwing, mosh-pitting, stage-diving fans may have them running for the door. But take anyone who likes music to Katatonia, one of the giants of the genre in the modern era, and it is likely that within a few songs they will at least be nodding their head. Another reason for the popularity of doom in the Middle East is that it is generally not as subversive as other genres. Many doom bands, including Black Sabbath, have dabbled with the occult and some political themes, but modern doom tends to focus more on life, misery and (usually lost) love.

Ahmed met another local metalhead, Ghassan, in a local music store in Jeddah back in 2003 and discovered a shared love not only of metal but of doom. They formed a band, recruiting members of Wasted Land and tossing around a number of potential names, including Weeping Winter and

Dark Vision, before settling on Grieving Age. By 2005 they had recorded their first single, 'My Hopeless River', drawing influence from doom bands such as My Dying Bride and the early material of British band Anathema. Ahmed's tortured, high-pitched shrieks are set against massive, leaden guitar riffs, with the shortest song on their album *Merely the Fleshless We and the Awed Obsequy* 15 minutes long and the longest almost half an hour.

In terms of style, everything about Grieving Age – from their music to their message – is as far from Creative Waste as it is possible to be, but their situation was largely the same. As a metal fan growing up in Jeddah, even the small metal scene was a big deal. Ahmed had only been able to get CDs by asking friends or family members travelling abroad to smuggle them into the country. Even as a budding musician, it was impossible to form a band because none of Saudi Arabia's metallers knew each other. While in other Middle East countries, such as Egypt and Lebanon, rock and metal fans coalesced around venues or record stores, few of these existed in austere Saudi Arabia.

Despite over a decade of playing together and recording albums, Grieving Age never performed in their home country. But that did not stop them practising regularly and flying to al-Khobar, on the east coast, to record in music studios. When CDs were pressed, they would be handed around amongst friends and occasionally sold by small distributors in Europe or elsewhere in the Middle East. It was a pared-down, DIY scene: "We were a small community. We knew how to keep it quiet and well organised," Ahmed said.

There had been at least one live gig in Jeddah in the 1990s. Hasan Hatrash, a local musician, remembered attending at a cafe downtown. But it was quickly shut down by the religious police and many of the organisers and crowd were arrested. "It lit the fire, that show. It was the beginning of pushing the boundaries."

After the raid, bands in Jeddah stopped organising shows in their homes or local cafes and instead began approaching the managers of expatriate compounds, where the bulk of the kingdom's wealthy foreign workers – many of them Americans – lived normal lives behind high walls and fortified guardhouses. Many of the compounds had bars that served alcohol and were willing to have local musicians play. Hasan's band, Most of Us, played at a compound in the Italian diplomatic quarter, in Jeddah's embassy district, later that year. "It was the most exhilarating, scary, beautiful feeling I have ever had in my life," he said.

But despite the odd gig, the scene remained low key in Jeddah until the early 2000s, when the internet arrived in Saudi Arabia and opened the floodgates for young people like Ahmed and Hasan. Not only could they access music, but they realised that metal scenes existed in other cities. In al-Khobar, a small group of metal fans were gathering regularly at the Adawliah music shop in the Rashid Mall. Bader Hussain, a Dammam-based metalhead, recalled that it was a middle-class, largely western-educated crowd from mostly liberal families in the major cities of the east coast:

> We got together into this small community where everyone spoke English. Even if I listened to Guns N' Roses and someone else listened to Cannibal Corpse, we had something in common. Today I know people can communicate online and there is a lot of openness, but when I was growing up there wasn't that. We used to gather at the music shop and stay there for hours playing instruments. We'd see a guy come in with an instrument and then we'd invite them to a metal jam.

In 2002, Kamal al-Nuaimi, the founder of Saudi band Deathless Anguish, began the 'SA Metal' message board, which allowed Saudi bands from across the country to speak to each other for the first time. Al-Nuaimi, who also played in Saudi band Sound of Ruby, organised a show in Dammam that year with Creative Waste that is generally agreed to be the first heavy metal show in Saudi Arabia. Shows not only provided opportunities to see live music but allowed musicians to share CDs and videos and broaden their knowledge of heavy metal when internet music sharing was still in its infancy. Fawaz remembers that after the gig he was given a stash of 20 music videos, including those by Carcass as well as by Seattle grunge band Silverchair: "It was very educational," he said.

The next live show that Creative Waste played was in Bahrain, the island state joined to Saudi Arabia via the King Fahd Causeway. Bahrain was a refuge for those escaping Saudi Arabia's strict rules on consuming alcohol and the mixing of the sexes and thousands of Saudis would drive across the causeway on Thursday nights to party in freewheeling Manama for the weekend.

Creative Waste shared the bill with two other Saudi bands, Deathless Anguish and Sound of Ruby, with 45-minute sets allotted apiece. But from the very beginning the show got off to a bad start. Most of the Bahraini bands were playing covers and "behaved like rock stars with chips on their shoulders," Fawaz recalled. When the Bahrainis overran, the organisers announced that the three Saudi bands actually had only 15 minutes for their sets and would have to play last on the bill, when many of the younger members of the crowd would have gone home. As Creative Waste got ready to play, members of the crowd shouted abuse and sarcastic comments about Saudis having low IQs.

When the music started, the Bahrainis stood at the back of the crowd impassively as the few Saudis who had made the journey showed support by headbanging by the stage. "We were treated like outsiders," Fawaz recalled. "As soon as we were setting up on stage and ready to perform, we could instantly feel this unwelcoming vibe from most of the crowd," he said. "After this show, we decided no more Bahrain; we'll do our own thing from now on."

The five years that followed would be remembered as a watershed for Saudi bands both in Jeddah and on the east coast. The SA Metal forum had brought musicians out of the woodwork and the successful show in Dammam had convinced those bands that remembered them that the bad old days were behind them. King Fahd, who began his rule as a 'playboy prince' but went on to become a deeply conservative and reactionary ruler, was still in power but was so incapacitated by the middle of the decade that King Abdullah was in effective ruler of the kingdom.

In Jeddah, Hasan played regularly in expatriate compounds. On the east coast, gigs were held in private villas at least once a year. Even though the bands had to jump through the hoops of the religious authorities in order not to get arrested, the scene grew and musicians came together like never before. "We always had to improvise to the best of our ability without alerting the authorities, mainly the religious police," said Fawaz. "We would band together with like-minded friends and organise do-it-yourself public gigs in private areas while still abiding by the rules – no mixed-gender gatherings and no alcohol – which helped build an extremely underground scene."

As well as the numerous small shows in people's houses or backyards, there were three major gigs organised by the metalheads who ran the SA Metal forum. The last of these was a concert that has become part of Saudi heavy metal history. Over 500 men turned out at an expatriate compound in al-Khobar for the gig headlined by Sound of Ruby, the veteran Jeddah band. As the venue had been rented for a private function and was in a compound, the bands were confident that they would escape the attention of the religious police. They clubbed together all their equipment, sold tickets to their friends, and built a stage. "We just rented an empty room. All of the equipment, even the cables, we had to borrow or buy. We set it all up ourselves," said Fawaz. Buoyed by its success, live shows followed in Riyadh and again in al-Khobar, and for a while it began to look like things were really changing in Saudi Arabia. Then, in June 2009, they did.

* * *

It was a hot summer afternoon in Riyadh when the dozen or so men arrived at an expatriate compound, their cars full of speakers, mic stands and amplifiers. As they tuned their guitars, tested mics and cracked jokes, an atmosphere of pre-gig excitement hung in the air. The organisers had been planning the show for weeks, but in Riyadh it was not like you could just put up posters in the street to advertise a heavy metal concert. Instead, the promoters had huge files of names, phone numbers and emails and sold tickets direct to fans.

The venue was in a compound on King Fahd Road, one of the main thoroughfares through the city. It had a limit of 300 people but for some reason the organisers had sold upwards of 700 tickets. Halfway through the show, the doormen stopped letting people in and an angry crowd gathered outside. Then someone called the religious police.

When they arrived, the gig was immediately shut down and the organisers, a local Saudi promoter and a Syrian expatriate, were arrested. The pair were held on a range of charges, from drug dealing to satanism, and thrown in jail. The Saudi promoter would eventually serve 12 months in prison and was never involved in the Saudi metal scene again. His Syrian accomplice was deported. The metal scene gave a collective shudder.

Neither Fawaz nor Bader were at the gig, but – like everyone else – they heard about it. By this point the pair had taken over the running of SA Metal from Nuaimi, but after Riyadh they decided enough was enough. The following night, Bader decided to end his role in the metal scene. "I went online and shut down everything," he explained. "I didn't want to get in trouble. I'd just got married; I had my job and my life. I didn't want problems because of the fault of others." Across the country, others followed his lead. Still today, the botched gig in Riyadh remains Saudi Arabia's last live metal show. "They got reckless, it has to be said," said Fawaz, "and it affected everyone."

Riyadh is a very different animal to the rest of Saudi Arabia's cities. It was little more than a dusty fort and a few hundred homes before the foundation of Saudi Arabia in 1932 by the warrior king Abdulaziz al-Saud, but has since been transformed into a massive urban sprawl of some 6 million people. Saudi Arabia's Eastern Province has been a booming oil region since the 1950s. Jeddah has a long history as an international port and hub for pilgrims. But Riyadh is Wahhabi-land, the birthplace of the ultraconservative religious sect that dominates Saudi Arabia, where the world's most austere form of Islam meets the rough Bedouin culture of the desert.

Even in Jeddah and al-Khobar, there were at least a couple of music stores and recording facilities: in Riyadh, there was nothing. Maybe that was why the organisers of the June 2009 show did what they did: if it had gone ahead without a hitch it would have been a groundbreaking event in the social history of Saudi heavy metal. But there is a reason why, of all of Saudi Arabia's heavy metal bands, not a single one was formed in the capital.

A year later, the Saudi scene had a second blow when MTV came to the kingdom to record a documentary, *True Life – Resist the Power, Saudi Arabia*, and interviewed a Jeddah band, Breeze of the Dying. A so-called 'metal-core' band – a genre that fused elements of hardcore and heavy metal – Breeze of the Dying had first played live at the ill-fated Riyadh show. Jude al-Dajani remembered that they had played four songs, one of which they had written only a few days before. "From the very beginning of our set, people were going nuts. It still gives me goose bumps."

When the band took part in the MTV interview, they discussed the issues with playing live but didn't touch on anything controversial. They even told the show that when they played live they would turn their band T-shirts inside out to avoid insulting Islam. But, sadly, the documentary was not only about Breeze of the Dying. It also interviewed a young man, Aziz, who was filmed trying to meet his girlfriend for a date, a strict taboo in Saudi Arabia, where unmarried or unrelated men and women are not permitted to go out in public together.

The result was explosive. Within days, a lawsuit had been filed against three of the youths in the film on charges of 'promoting sin', and although the charges were not pursued, it was another shot across the bows for Saudi metallers. Jude felt misled by the documentary makers and regretted that Breeze of the Dying had taken part, even if it did serve to make the band's name outside Saudi Arabia. "We had high hopes as kids that MTV would show Saudi as a great place to live in. Show all the great places and communities we have here. However, they went with a different angle," he said.

Jude had met Breeze of the Dying's guitarist, Khalid, via the SA Metal forum and quickly recruited other friends to fill other positions in the band, including Khalid's brother, Majed. "We had our first live show in a small backyard of a rental house, which bands usually rented out to play shows. It was a successful night," Jude recalled. "We were young, energetic, and full of talent. We had a different flavour to our music than the other melodic death and death metal bands." But it was the Riyadh show that made Breeze of the Dying's name. "After that show, our name was on the lips of every metalhead," he said.

Jude had first got into heavy metal after he heard his sister listening to music:

> I had never heard such loudness. I went in her
> room, and saw her headbanging. I asked her what
> the hell are you listening to? And she told me it
> was Nirvana. From then on I was set free to roam
> the world of rock and metal music. It made me feel
> energetic, focused, and spoke to my emotions.

It helped that his family were early supporters of his passion. His mother would often sit with him in their house in Jeddah and listen to Metallica, and, after they formed Breeze of the Dying, his grandfather built a stage at the family beach house outside Jeddah. The authorities were not so easy to win over. Breeze of the Dying had regular private shows in the years following their debut in Riyadh, and were often raided by the police. But they were usually only interested in looking for alcohol or drugs, neither of which the band would tolerate at their gigs. When they didn't find any contraband, they would leave them alone.

Despite the country's conservatism, Saudi Arabia's metal scene has not been targeted by accusations of satanism in the same way that metalheads have been in Egypt, Lebanon and Syria. When gigs in the kingdom were shut down, it was usually for infractions such as mixing of the sexes or rules against gatherings of more than 50 people. As long as Saudi Arabia's metallers managed to stay below the radar, they have generally been tolerated by the police. There certainly has been nothing of the kind of media hysteria that has rocked Egypt or the Levant.

But the diversity of the Middle East has always been reflected in its heavy metal scene. Many of the metal bands – or indeed bands of all genres – from Lebanon and Egypt consider themselves atheists, or at least non-religious, reflecting the fact that both countries are multi-denominational, home to Christians, Muslims and non-believers. While Lebanese bands such as Ayat and Damaar kept a low profile, extreme bands were able to play live in Lebanon. Many advertised their gigs, sold CDs openly and played live shows semi-regularly, even if they were openly anti-religious. But in theocracies such as Saudi Arabia and Iran, metal musicians are rarely openly critical of faith. Iran has a thriving black metal scene, but its bands are rarely attracted to the irreligious and satanic message of European and American bands.

In Saudi Arabia, the dynamic is the same. While, in the West, the vast majority of extreme metal bands are either ambivalent to religion or outrightly against it, in Saudi Arabia it is the other way around. Most Saudi metallers reject those within the scene who openly disrespect religion and black metal bands like Dimmu Borgir, which are massive in other parts of the Middle East, do not have a big following in the kingdom. Ask Saudi metallers about black metal and they are generally contemptuous of it, seeing it not only as offensive but also as creating problems for metal bands who are not anti-religious. In other scenes, metalheads may not play black metal but still respect it and even listen to it privately, but in Saudi Arabia it is seen as anathema to what heavy metal fans stand for. Majed, from Breeze of the Dying, said:

> People see that stuff and they think we are all like that. The authorities have always hated metal music and stuff like that gives them an excuse to act against us. They see these people on the internet and they say: "This is metal music. This is what you

believe in." Satanism and upside-down crosses. I mean, what the fuck? That's not metal. It's these people who cause all the problems.

But the issue is also about faith. A majority of Saudi Arabia's relatively small metal scene identify as Muslims and see no contradiction between that and their passion for extreme music. This is often reflected in their choice of genres: while the majority of black metal has been mostly anti-religion and often outright satanic, death metal has tended instead to focus on horror movies and gore. Grindcore is often political, but it can also simply be irreverent and offensive. Creative Waste may take aim at corruption and poverty, but they do not sing about Islam.

Meanwhile, the subgenre of heavy metal known as doom – which is where Jeddah's Grieving Age fall on the musical spectrum – is rarely anti-religion: bands such as Katatonia and My Dying Bride sing about love, life and loss. The rolling, immersive riffs are about escapism, not rage. When Ahmed, Grieving Age's frontman, is asked about the connection between the music he plays and his faith, he is defensive: "Metal is music. What has religion got to do with it?"

Jude, from Breeze of the Dying, was raised a Muslim and he hates that dogmatic conservatism is preventing many young Saudis from getting into metal. "I was brought up in a house that taught me Islam is a peaceful and easy-going religion. Music is not harmful; it is more peaceful nowadays, especially with all the religious wars and politics going on. You look to music as an escape route or even, to some, as a religion itself," he said. "But it is still hard for young kids in metal bands to speak out and be proud of what they do. They find it difficult to mention that they play in a metal band, because of what society will think of them."

This is not to say that there is no anti-Islamic black metal in Saudi Arabia, or indeed in the wider Middle East. Over the years, a number of bands have emerged that claim to be from countries such as Saudi Arabia, Bahrain and Iraq and belong to a loose coalition of bands called the Arabic Anti-Islamic Legion. Facts about these bands are hard to come by, given that most of them are anonymous and only communicate with journalists online. In 2012 it was claimed that one band, Janaza, was fronted by a 28-year-old woman from Iraq who had released an album called *Burn the Pages of the Koran*. 'Anahita' gave only two interviews, and, speaking to *The Atlantic*, said that she was raised in a Muslim household in Baghdad until her parents and brother were killed in a suicide bombing. Her brutal, low-fi music, reminiscent of the earliest Norwegian black metal, is still available on YouTube. As with all great black metal, most of the lyrics are unintelligible – apart from the song's chorus, Anahita screaming "Burn the Fucking Koran" over and over again. Another band, Seeds of Iblis – which has songs such as 'No Koran' and 'Allah is Dead' – is also believed to come from Iraq, while another, Tadnees, whose named translates as 'desecration' and whose songs include 'Nuke Mecca', claims to be from Saudi Arabia.

Perhaps it is not a surprise that of all the countries these bands could come from it would be Iraq and Saudi Arabia. Islam itself was a product of the violence of sixth-century Arabia: Mohammed and his followers wanted to tame that world, to bring it order. Wahhabi Islam took those teachings and then twisted them to accommodate the harsh tribal life of the desert, in a crude fusion of the Quran and Bedouin tribal politics. The music of bands such as Tadnees, Seeds of Iblis and Janaza is black metal at its purest: flat-out, violent, relentless and repetitive. It is cathartic – and what people are in more need of catharsis than those living either under the Wahhabi faith or in war-torn twenty-first-century Iraq?

There has been much speculation over the years that the Arabic Anti-Islamic Legion is a hoax, dreamed up in a bedroom in California or Oslo, cobbled together out of images and recordings of unknown bands and packaged together for the social media age. These rumours have been driven by the fact that black metal bands are notoriously secretive even in Europe, let alone in countries where their message could get them a death sentence. But while it may be difficult to confirm the existence of anti-Islamic black metal, it is easy to imagine where it comes from – and why.

Mephisto, the frontman in Saudi black metal band al-Namrood – which literally translates as 'non-believer' – keeps such a low profile that he will not reveal his real name, his age or any information that could lead to his being identified. Al-Namrood are one of only two metal bands from Saudi Arabia that are openly anti-religious, and the only one whose existence I have been able to verify.

Mephisto claims to draw his influence from pre-Islamic philosophy and proclaims an absolute rejection of Islam. Despite being veritable outcasts on the Middle East metal scene for the trouble that they cause, al-Namrood draw heavily from traditional Middle Eastern music, incorporating instruments such as the oud and the ney, a traditional Arabic flute. Their 2015 album *Diaji al-Joor* starts with a dissonant, acoustic track that uses traditional instruments before fast-picked oud gives way to the tremolo-picked guitars of black metal. Later in the album, the chugging guitars and blast-beat drums are joined again by an oud. Other than Melechesh, the Jerusalem black metal band, few Middle Eastern bands fuse European metal and traditional Arab music so effectively.

Mephisto grew up in Saudi Arabia in the early 1990s at the time of the war in Yugoslavia, and remembers clearly the effect that graphic videos of Serbian atrocities against Bosnian Muslims had on Saudi society. He was shown footage of the conflict in class and encouraged to go abroad and fight jihad. "They told us: 'See what they are doing to Muslims, you should all grow up with hatred and bring revenge to your brothers in Islam,'" he said. "They taught us we shall not have any positive emotion toward the non-Muslim, even if they were kind to us, even if they treat us in hospitals and save our lives we should not be grateful. Many children really felt outrage towards non-Muslims." His contempt for Islam was only intensified when school friends followed the advice and travelled overseas to fight jihad.

Mephisto met the other two members of al-Namrood, Osron and Humbaba, at a party and was shocked to have met like-minded musicians by chance in a country like Saudi Arabia. They remained guarded about their political and religious beliefs until they knew each other well.

Mephisto, who is the band's guitarist, said he grew up listening to Iron Maiden, whose demonic Eddie mascot and songs like 'Number of the Beast' provoked him to start looking into more extreme genres of heavy metal. "We rejected religion from an early age. It didn't make sense to us, we didn't like the forcing of religion on one's life," he said.

As adults, all three members of the band have to maintain the ruse that they are practising Muslims, including pretending to pray when they are corralled into mosques by friends, colleagues or even the religious police. "We play along, we never tend to attract any other views on us, other than we are just regular Muslims. We know what to say, what the people want to hear and what we should do. It became routine." At least one member of the band has served time in jail – although Mephisto will not reveal when or what for – and as a result the band cannot leave Saudi Arabia. If they could, he said, they would. Unlike many black metal bands, Al-Namrood are not satanists; rather, they are anti-religious and anarchist and their focus is on pre-Islamic cultures that have traditionally been ignored, if not vilified, in Saudi Arabia.

Mephisto, unsurprisingly, is not optimistic that their music will ever be allowed in Saudi Arabia – nor that the country will ever change substantially from the fanatical theocracy that it is today. They cite the example of Raif Badawi, the blogger who was arrested and publicly lashed for writing a blog that the authorities claim questioned the existence of God, as evidence of why they have to guard their secrecy so jealously. "Raif Badawi was arrested because he was a blogger writing about liberty and people's rights: so how would they react to our music?" he said.

* * *

The Arab Spring shocked Saudi Arabia's rulers to the core and Riyadh did all it could to undermine the revolutions in Egypt, Tunisia and Libya. The protests in Qatif, while initially pro-democracy, could not fail to take on a sectarian dimension, as an almost entirely Shia movement against a Sunni monarchy. Riyadh helped put down the revolution in Bahrain and gave millions to General Abdel Fattah el-Sisi after he overthrew Mohammed Morsi in Egypt.

When, on 23 January 2015, King Abdullah died and was replaced by his brother, Salman, hopes of further reform in Saudi Arabia initially receded: Salman was a conservative, considered close to the Wahhabi establishment that had hated Abdullah for his efforts to open up Saudi Arabia. But there have been positive moves from the new king. In early 2016, Salman stripped the religious police of their powers of arrest. No longer could the Committee for the Promotion of Virtue and the Prevention of Vice roam the streets arresting women for not covering their hair or corralling men into mosques at prayer time.

For Saudi musicians, who had suffered under the religious police for decades, the decision was a watershed. "Six years ago we couldn't do a metal show because of the religious police, but now they don't have the same authority like before – now they are just like a public relations agency. This is the best improvement ever," said Bader.

In the decade since that gig, Bader had moved to Riyadh, where he now lives with his wife and a two-and-a-half-year-old son and runs a successful marketing agency. Even his tastes have mellowed; now he listens to progressive metal bands like Opeth and Mouth of the Architect rather than Cannibal Corpse and Deicide. But he sees genuine change in Saudi Arabia. In the business world he now inhabits, he regularly sees Saudi women speaking at events and taking roles as executives in companies – for Saudi Arabia, that is a revelation. It is early days, because people are apprehensive, but times are changing. "People can now go with their female friends to restaurants and have dinner. But many haven't realised that yet. They were born with a fear of the religious police," he said.

Hasan Hatrash, the Jeddah musician who attended the city's first gig in 1995, agreed. He is now in his early forties and has a perspective that some of the younger members of the scene don't. He attributes much of the change in mindset to the internet, which has meant that Saudi Arabia's conservative elements can no longer block out the world and hope it goes away. In the old days, Saudi musicians could only get hold of new CDs and tapes either when friends would smuggle them in or when embassy officials and foreign workers would trade them with locals. This meant that only the very well connected or the wealthy could get hold of new music, let alone books, newspapers and art.

I am surprised at the speed and pace of the openness that is happening in this society. What we needed was the interaction with the others so we could open their minds, and that happened. The internet is in every house now. There is a cell phone in every rabbit hole.

Hasan has always dressed in an alternative way; he has had long hair since he was a teenager. But nowadays he barely warrants a second look when he strolls down a Jeddah street with his guitar slung over his shoulder. "Nobody ever looks at me twice. In the 1990s or the 2000s I would attract all this attention. Now this look is extremely normal. Even I am surprised. It shocks me how fast it happened. You see a lot of people with long hair, looking hip," he said. There has even been an increasing trend of young Saudis getting tattoos – a serious social and religious issue because it is forbidden in the Quran. "That would have been heresy," Hasan said.

But Hasan does not see his future in Saudi Arabia. The next generation may benefit from the new period of openness that plenty see in Saudi Arabia in the era of King Salman, but Hasan is sick of waiting. The fall in oil prices that began in 2014 and continued into 2017 seriously hit his business as a journalist. At the same time there remains no institution for art and his love of film and music has few outlets. "When I said we're open I didn't mean that we are healthily open. We are still in the first stage of openness. We might need another decade or two to be kind of normal. So for me, by that time

I will be too old to do shit. That is where my concern is. If I was younger than this, I would see the potential," he said. Hasan is looking to New Zealand, a place he has never been to, as a new potential home. "I am a hippy, I am chilled, and to me that place kind of provides that. Even if World War Three erupted, in New Zealand we wouldn't even know about it. It's a place for me to stay peacefully, away from this fucked-up world that we are living in," he said.

Jude left Saudi Arabia soon after the furore of the MTV show and moved to Boston, where he joined a local band, Wrathsputin, and toured a number of venues in the US. In 2016 he returned to Saudi Arabia and got in touch with his former Breeze of the Dying bandmates. Even when he lived in the US he had been writing music for the band, and he has since hit the studio to record a new EP.

Back in Saudi, he passes the time working for IKEA and running a cat and dog rescue charity and a wrestling podcast. He is optimistic that King Salman is serious about making changes to Saudi society that might make it easier for Breeze of the Dying. "But we need to test the waters before we start doing shows again," he said. Like many Saudi metallers, he misses the scene of the 2000s and rues the fact that many of the old crowd have moved on:

Metal music is not as popular as it used to be in the early 2000s. It is still considered the devil's music in a lot of homes. Metal has reached an all-time low here. Our shows back then had 100 to 300 people coming, it was insane, but basically everyone who attended the shows back then or listened to metal music is now into electronic music.

Jude doesn't see any young bands coming through. There is still a lack of music education in Saudi Arabia, and the lack of options to play together and perform naturally hinders people from improving as musicians. There is also a natural scepticism from all but the most liberal families about music – particularly heavy metal music – not only because of its association with irreligious ideas but because it is seen as a waste of time. And there remains a chronic lack of drummers, Jude reflected bitterly, making it extremely difficult to get a serious band together. Even if you do, there are few places to practise and no venues to play gigs.

But Jude doesn't see the problem as being specific to Saudi Arabia; he sees the metal scene across the world as a pale imitation of what it was in the 1980s and 1990s. "It is just too disgusting to listen to. Look at the 1980s, when metal was Megadeth and Metallica, and the 1990s when we had grunge. It is a rollercoaster, of course, but looking at it now I see that the rock and metal carts are falling downhill."

* * *

As for Fawaz, Creative Waste remains his focus even as the guys get older and he looks to a new life overseas with his wife, a Spanish metalhead who he met at a gig in Bahrain. He said that the prospect for compound gigs, once a lifeline for Saudi bands, has fallen away. With the rise of terrorism and ISIS and suicide attacks in the Eastern Province, expatriate compounds have closed their doors and are reluctant to allow ordinary Saudis to arrange gigs. "They have to let you in their circle and they don't want to do that," he said.

As for the changes to Saudi society, such as the neutering of the religious police, Fawaz said he is yet to see the effect. In the big cities, Hasan and Bader may see the effects of reforms, but in a rundown Shia-majority city like Qatif, change comes slowly. Saudi Arabia's middle classes are experiencing new freedoms, but further down the social scale things are harder. "We keep reading these articles about how the religious police are stripped of their arresting powers, but places still close for prayer times. They say they are trying to revive culture, but I don't see anything concrete."

Then there are the security challenges with living in Qatif, which has become a target of jihadi groups, including ISIS. But even those risks do not concern Fawaz as much as the day-to-day challenges of living in Saudi Arabia. "We have a lot of things to worry about," he said. "The least of our worries are the goddamn terrorists."

CHAPTER 5
ISRAEL AND PALESTINE

Tamer Nafar never really understood hip hop until he heard Tupac Shakur. As a teenager, he'd heard rap as part of other songs – Michael Jackson's 1991 hit 'Jam' or 'Informer' by Snow – but he'd never really got it until he managed to get a copy of Tupac's 'White Man'z World'. The lyrics, which document Tupac's violent life on the streets of Los Angeles, couldn't help but chime with a 16-year-old from Lod, known as Israel's Murder City. "I was like: 'Wow, this is fucking different,'" he said. "I was stunned."

Even in the 1990s, before the violence of the Second Intifada and the wars in Gaza, Lod was a crime-ridden city where drive-by shootings and fights between rival gangs were a daily occurrence. Once a thriving trade stop on the road between Jaffa and Jerusalem, Lod – then called Lydda and still known today as Lyd by the Palestinians – had witnessed some of the worst excesses of the Zionist militias in 1948 as they fought to carve an Israeli state from the British Mandate of Palestine. Fifty years later, Arabs were a minority in Lod, living in run-down neighbourhoods where sewage ran in the streets and Palestinian families were packed into ramshackle houses on the bad side of town. Palestinian gangs fought amongst themselves for control of the drugs trade as the Israeli police force turned a blind eye. To get to the Palestinian part of town from the train station, residents had to walk across the sleepers. The Arab neighbourhood of Lod was quite literally on the wrong side of the tracks.

The band that Tamer formed in the late 1990s, DAM, became legendary across the Middle East and eventually the world, sharing stages with everyone from Wu-Tang Clan to Dead Prez and Talib Kweli. As the first Palestinian group to rap in Arabic, DAM would inspire a generation of Arab rappers living in Israel, the West Bank and Gaza, as well as from Egypt, Syria and everywhere in between. But it all began in Lod, with a teenage Tamer sat on his bed, listening to Tupac, and flipping through his Arabic–English dictionary in an effort to understand every line. "I became obsessed," he said. In the days before the internet, Tamer would frequently stumble over the gritty American slang of Tupac's lyrics. He resorted to approaching the only black people he ever saw in Israel, Ethiopian Jews, to ask if they understood words like 'homie' and 'Gs'. On reflection, he said, it was racist. But he was fascinated. He had to know.

It was not long before Tamer corralled his brother, Suheil, into working with him, and in 1998 the pair recorded their first single, 'Stop Selling Drugs'. They held a launch party in the garden of his house where a friend introduced Tamer to Mahmoud Jreri, who lived nearby and shared a love of Tupac. The trio began rapping in English and then in Hebrew, a language in which they were all fluent, and started performing in Tel Aviv as part of a growing Israeli hip hop scene.

Then Tamer decided to try rapping in Arabic. Unlike in Hebrew and English, where there were numerous artists to imitate, he was starting from scratch. "It took a while for my body and my tongue to feel the delivery and the flow: the way of writing, the way to approach it. How do you make it sound like it isn't subtitled? How do you make it sound original? It took time." Tamer released his first Arabic song, 'Ta lal alef la MER' ('T to the A to the MER'), and immediately found an audience: "Hebrew and English didn't work. But as soon as I dropped my first Arabic single, I got a crowd."

DAM were always a political band. As Palestinians born in Israel they were classed as Israeli citizens, which meant that they could move relatively freely around the country and travel abroad on Israeli passports. Not that life was always that easy for Israel's 1.6 million 'Israeli Arabs'. The Palestinian community in Israel has long been subject to discrimination and is disproportionately affected by issues such as unemployment, double the rate of Jewish Israelis. Even though Palestinian citizens of Israel can travel through

Ben Gurion Airport on their Israeli passports, many prefer to go via Jordan in light of the treatment they suffer at the hands of immigration officials. The fact that DAM discussed these issues won them fans who may not have ordinarily listened to hip hop.

Palestinian music is traditionally centred around *dabke* – the folk dance that is seen at Arab weddings and celebrations across the Levant – and the classical Arabic singers who became popular after 1948. DAM took the messages of the Palestinian struggle and fused them with the beats of modern rappers like Biggie Smalls and Tupac. As a result, even today older Palestinians are fans. "The older generation say they don't listen to hip hop," said Tamer, "but they listen to DAM."

By 2001, the band was firmly established on both the Arabic and the international music scene, lauded in the media and at the centre of a growing Palestinian hip hop circuit. More and more young rappers, with access to music via the internet, began to form groups and record. DAM didn't just convert young and old Palestinians to hip hop; they also attracted fans from across the Arab world, particularly in the massive Palestinian diaspora in Lebanon, Jordan and the Gulf. In the West, DAM made headlines in US and European newspapers, where the sight of three Arabs in baggy trousers and backward caps performing hip hop was a novelty – even if most readers did not understand Arabic.

But their rising popularity came alongside something else: a period of violence that would change Israel and Palestine and come to define a new generation of Arabs and Jews. Where tensions had once simmered, they would boil. Where anger had once lain dormant, it would explode. Within a few years of DAM's formation, the streets of Tel Aviv and Jerusalem, Jenin and Nablus, would be gripped by conflict. Palestinian suicide bombers would kill hundreds of civilians in packed nightclubs and on buses. Israeli air strikes would turn Palestinian cities into rubble. In the coming war, everyone would be forced to take a side. For many Palestinians, DAM would be their soundtrack.

* * *

Across the Middle East, only a handful of heavy metal bands are considered to have 'made it' – and first among them is Jerusalem's Melechesh. Founded in 1993 as a solo project, the band has travelled the world and recorded four EPs and six albums. Its founder, Ashmedi, has toured with bands he grew up listening to, including Exodus, Anthrax and Sepultura. But Ashmedi, an Armenian with a Turkish passport, is still reluctant to be seen as a brand ambassador for a country that doesn't consider him a citizen:

> When I say that people think we are 'self-hating' or whatever, but it's not that. I have the right to my

identity. If the Israelis gave me a passport and I was part of the legal system, then call me whatever you want. But that's not the case, so why should other people get credit for us?

Ashmedi's Christian grandfather lost his entire family during the Armenian genocide, only surviving because his Muslim neighbours took him in and raised him as their own. After he married, the family moved to Aleppo, where Ashmedi's mother was born, and then to Israel. She met his father, a Christian Turk who had also settled in Israel, and the pair were married in Jerusalem. His father opened a tailor shop in the narrow streets of the Arab quarter where Ashmedi and his brother were born.

Then, when Ashmedi was five months old, his father was killed in a car crash. His mother was left with a seven-year-old and a five-month-old baby, managing a men's tailor's in a male-dominated society with a dozen employees. Nonetheless, Ashmedi remembered his mother handling the situation well. He grew up in a happy home in an Arab neighbourhood. "I learned Arabic in the neighbourhood with the Palestinians; they helped raise me," he said. Jerusalem was not yet synonymous with violence and religious fanaticism, and Ashmedi remembered the city as liberal, tolerant and inclusive. "Christian or Muslim, no one cared in those days," he said.

Although based in Jerusalem, the family still made regular trips to the US, including Los Angeles, where Ashmedi was exposed to the emerging thrash scene. When the first Gulf War broke out in 1990 and Saddam Hussein's scud missiles rained down on Israel, the family briefly moved to Miami, where the 15-year-old Ashmedi first saw Slayer. By the time he returned, what had been a tiny death metal scene in Jerusalem had exploded.

There were still no bars that would play metal in Jerusalem – let alone venues that would host metal bands – so rock fans would gather at Zion Square in the west of the city and hang out and talk about music. Once a month a local club would hold a metal night and fans would pack into the venue and headbang to whatever was being played. Then they would head to a nearby games arcade or back to Zion Square. "We'd sit in the square and drink arak – or whatever we could afford. And that was it. That was the Jerusalem scene."

When they wanted a change they would take the bus down to Tel Aviv, where there were more metal shops and a handful of venues, some of which hosted international acts, including UK bands like Napalm Death and Carcass. After the gig, they would head to the beach and wait until dawn, when the buses started. "We'd hang out until sunrise and then go back to Jerusalem."

After a year on the Jerusalem scene, Ashmedi joined a death metal band and played a few shows, but the global explosion of grunge in the US in the early 1990s found its way to Israel and many heavy metal fans crossed over. "A lot of guys who had long hair cut it off and got undercuts," he said.

In 1993 Ashmedi started Melechesh as a one-man project, joined the following year by his guitarist, Moloch, and drummer, Lord Curse. At the time there was only one black metal band in Israel, but it was based in Tel Aviv, a traditionally liberal and secular city that, if not amenable to the genre's more outrageous irreligious elements, at least tolerated them. Jerusalem, the seat of the three Abrahamic faiths and home to pious believers from Orthodox Jews to Palestinian Muslims to Christians of every denomination and sect, was a different story. Before long, Melechesh were the most notorious band in Jerusalem.

In the early 1990s, the metal scene was almost exclusively Israeli. A few western expatriates would turn up at shows, but Palestinian fans would not. The venues were all in Jewish West Jerusalem, and Arabs were rarely welcome.

> People were more racist then than they are now.
> Maybe in Haifa or in Jaffa it was OK but in
> Jerusalem it was completely segregated. If Arabs
> wanted to go to West Jerusalem they would speak
> in English and wouldn't mention that they were
> Arabs. If the Israelis in the crowd heard Arabic it
> was like witchcraft – their smiles would change.

The same went for bands. As of 2017, there have been only two Palestinian metal bands – Chaos of Nazareth and Khalas – but their members are from Nazareth and Acre, inside Israel. Ashmedi had a Turkish passport and was Armenian, but it was often assumed he was Palestinian because he spoke fluent Arabic. Moloch, Melechesh's guitarist, is Palestinian-Assyrian.

But regardless of their ethnicity, the sight of Ashmedi and Moloch dressed in their black clothes with their piercings, spiked bracelets and long hair raised eyebrows in Arab East Jerusalem. "It was weird for them. They didn't know what to make of it," he said. Their notoriety had benefits though: when parents in Jerusalem warned their daughters to stay away from Ashmedi, it always tended to have the opposite effect: "They liked bad boys," he said.

In the early days of Melechesh, the band was just beginning to master the sound that they would become famous for over the next two decades. Their first full-length album, *As Jerusalem Burns*, is fast, furious and fundamentally old school black metal. Ashmedi's voice is a high-pitched scream, Moloch's guitar work is fast-picked and treble-heavy, and Lord Curse's drums are mostly blast beats. Melechesh's song titles – 'Desert Pentagram' and 'As Jerusalem Burns' – were irreligious but the band was more interested in Sumerian and Assyrian mythology than in satanism.

But they still attracted unwanted attention from the media. A journalist for one of Israel's largest newspapers began following Ashmedi around, trying to persuade him to speak to him for a story, at one point offering him money. Eventually he relented (although he turned down the money) and told the reporter about black metal and the band's interest in the occult and mythology. He expressly stated that Melechesh were not satanists, but it was a point that the reporter chose to ignore.

When the newspaper ran the interview under the headline 'Satanic Cult', the Israeli police began cracking down on anyone on the metal scene who wore black clothes, pentagrams or spikes. Ashmedi was 18 and found himself classed as a 'person of interest' by the authorities. When he and Moloch were at the bus station or walking in the street, passers-by would stop their cars and shout "Satanic cult" from their windows. "Hell, I would be in town and girls would come up to me and be like: 'I want to join the cult.' I would be like: 'What cult? There is no cult. We are just four guys playing music!'"

But while the outrage had its funny side, it was also dangerous. Having a Turkish rather than an Israeli passport had its upsides – Ashmedi was not required to serve in the military, for example – but it also effectively meant that he could be deported at any time. "Israel is very tolerant to Israelis. You can shout at the prime minister and call him by his first name. But I am not an Israeli citizen so it was a fine line to tread," he said. To escape the heat, Ashmedi took a short holiday to Indonesia to visit his brother, who was then working in Jakarta, and by the time he returned the Israeli press had far more important things to write about.

That year, Israeli Prime Minister Yitzhak Rabin was gunned down at a rally in Tel Aviv, less than a year after agreeing a peace deal with Palestinian leader Yasser Arafat, for which both men won the Nobel Peace Prize. As Israel and Palestine began the slide into violence that would culminate in the Second Intifada, the negative attention paid by both the media and the authorities to metal bands such as Melechesh eased off. Melechesh featured in a documentary that was shown in Israel and the local media began to cover their new album launches and shows.

Melechesh had already recorded *As Jerusalem Burns …*, and they recorded a promo album, *Mesopotamian Metal*. But in a small country far from the heavy metal heartlands of Europe and the US, there was only ever so far that Melechesh could go in Israel. Ashmedi wanted more, and so he left Jerusalem for Holland.

*   *   *

It was early 1996 and the crowd at the Incubator, Tel Aviv, was a sea of mohawks and fists. At least 300 young punks packed into the tiny room: boots and braces, spit and rage.

Ishay Berger was 16, and on stage with Useless ID, a skater-punk band from Haifa. He had joined the band a few months earlier and was a good deal younger than the other members, who had cars and girlfriends and were well known on the tight-knit Israeli punk scene. "I felt like the luckiest kid in the world," he said. "We looked up to Useless ID as if they were NOFX or something. These guys were the real deal for us."

The band was told they had to perform first, and, as they took to the stage, the adrenaline was surging. In front of them was an angry, baying crowd: they weren't in Haifa anymore. "Once we got on that stage, I was flying. I was totally having the time of my life. But it didn't last long."

In Hebrew slang, an *ars* is a bully, a violent person of low class, a hooligan, a 'chav' or a 'redneck'. An 'arso punk' was a bully who had channelled that propensity for violence and aggression through the medium of flat-out angry British punk rock. Arso punk was a scene within a scene, and its adherents were known for trashing venues and fighting with the crowds and each other. The fans worshipped the boisterous music of UK bands such as Exploited, and any show they attended would generally degenerate into a chaotic, drunken mess of bodies, beer and blood.

That night at the Incubator, as the four regular-looking punk kids who made up Useless ID began to play, the arso punks unleashed their fury. "Before we knew it, there must have been a good 50-plus people spitting at us," Ishay said. By the end of the set, he was berating the crowd down a microphone: "I remember telling them that we will still be playing after they all drop out of punk and have regular, shitty boring lives." He was right. Within a few years, Useless ID had become one of Israel's most famous bands, signed to a label owned by NOFX's Fat Mike and touring with groups that they had idolised as kids back in Haifa.

After the show, Useless ID did all they could to avoid the arso punk scene but they formed a bond with Nekhei Na'atza, a veteran Israeli anarcho-punk band who were also on the bill that night. Nekhei Na'atza's set was fast, angry, political punk rock influenced by 1980s bands like Dead Kennedys and Minor Threat. "It was life-changing for me. I thought: if they could make me feel like that, then punk rock is probably more serious than I ever thought music could be," Ishay said.

Nekhei Na'atza began taking Useless ID along to shows across the country, including to Tel Aviv's legendary venue, Roxane, which had a capacity of over 1,000 and had hosted international bands such as Napalm Death, Biohazard and Radiohead. Even back then, most of the crowds would be death metal fans. "We were a minority inside a minority and it was pretty safe to say that even at a punk show you ended up hanging out with more metal kids than punk kids. There were just so many more of them," Ishay said.

In 1997, Nekhei Na'atza put out a seven-inch compilation of six Israeli punk bands, and Ishay played in three of them. By then, the scene in Israel was tight-knit. "After a show in Haifa, we had punks from Tel Aviv sleeping on our floors and vice versa. We would make tapes for each other and take good care of our friends. There was a good feeling that we were getting it right and fighting a good fight," he said.

As a movement, punk has traditionally been anti-authority, anti-religion and anti-war, and the Israeli scene was no different. Nekhei Na'atza's 1994 EP was titled *Renounce Judaism* and the band was openly anti-Zionist. "We despised the idea of Israel as a Jewish as well as a militaristic state," said Federico Gomez, the band's lead singer.

Federico and his brother, Santiago, had moved to Israel at the age of 11 from their native Argentina to a socialist kibbutz called Lehavot Habashan in Upper Galilee, close to the border with Lebanon and Syria. The kibbutz was isolated and Federico remembers that most of the other kids were still listening to 1960s and 1970s bands like Foreigner, Pink Floyd and Dire Straits, even as young people in the cities were getting swept up in the new wave scene, listening to The Cure and The Smiths as well as early punk rock. He read about punk in the Spanish music magazines that would occasionally be circulated amongst other young Spanish-speaking Jews in the kibbutz, and converted his brother to The Clash, The Ramones and The Sex Pistols.

At the beginning, that was as far as it went. Israel was culturally isolated in the late 1980s and the brothers were living in a remote socialist agricultural village, far from the cities of Haifa and Tel Aviv. But the one advantage of the kibbutz was that international post was free, and so Federico and Santiago began writing letters – first to fan clubs and teen magazines that occasionally found their way to Galilee and then to Alternative Tentacles, the UK distributors of Dead Kennedy's 1988 album *Frankenchrist*.

The label was run by a British artist, John Yates, who replied immediately with a newsletter that had addresses for dozens of other UK punk bands. "We sent letters to every address there and most answered and sent back mostly tapes, zines and leaflets. Then we sent letters to the new addresses that we found there and it kept growing until pretty much the end of the 1990s. We probably sent several letters a day the first three years or so we got into punk."

Federico, Santiago and their friend Oded Tal wrote to everyone from small punk rock outfits in Wales and Sheffield in the UK to bands from Japan, Canada and Germany. They would receive tapes and LPs in return, which they then copied and handed out to the few other punks they knew in Israel. In Europe and the US, letter writing between punks was usually in order to trade tapes or zines, but Federico and Santiago had little to offer. "Most were so surprised to get letters from Israel that they didn't seem to mind; they sent things anyway – they only asked for the stamps back and a blank cassette," Federico said.

The zines that would drop into the Gomez post box from the US and the UK were full of the radical political message then spreading on the punk scene through the lyrics of bands like Dead Kennedys, and the attitudes chimed with the socialist, anti-capitalist stance of their parents. "My brother and I came from a very politically conscious family, so a lot of the critique of capitalism found within punk fanzines and lyrics wasn't something totally new to us. But we became interested in anarchism as well as animal rights," he said. "We became vegetarians about a year after we started writing to punks abroad."

When Nekhei Na'atza became a band, they began receiving letters from young punks from other parts of Israel: "We started to get literally hundreds of letters from kids in Israel thirsty for information concerning radical politics, animal rights and punk," he said. It was these kids who flocked to their shows in the mid-1990s. "I do think that some Israeli teenagers and young people had similar ideas as ours, were against Israeli oppression of Palestine, wanted a secular state, and thought we somehow expressed also their own feelings," he said. But even the right-wing punks on the scene put up with Nekhei Na'atza's politics because, Federico guessed: "We were a good band to slam to."

The division between the hard-drinking and fight-loving arso punks and the peacenik political scene was only one source of animosity between sections of the Israeli scene; another major divide was over military service. Israel requires all citizens to serve three years in the armed forces once they turn 18. Depending on the decade, this could either mean manning patrols and raiding Palestinian homes in the West Bank and Gaza or fighting in an all-out war with one of Israel's neighbours. Even for Nekhei Na'atza, with their anti-state, anti-militaristic politics, the band was divided over whether to serve: "Of the seven people who were members of Nekhei Na'atza at one time or other, only two served in the army, which I guess is a very good percentage for Israel," Federico said.

The decision to serve or not is not only political; opting out of the army generally involves serving a jail term and can have a life-long impact on a young Israeli. Refusing to be conscripted can make it difficult to get jobs, even into adulthood, and is met with serious disapproval by relatives and the older generation of Israelis who fought in the conflicts of 1948, 1967 and 1973. As a result, most punk bands became established during their early teens before fading into obscurity once the members got drafted.

Nekhei Na'atza's stance on military service was influential on other young punks who didn't want to serve, although Federico said that it was easier to refuse in the

1990s than it is now. "Refusing to go to the army is still taboo for a lot of people. But being outspoken against the army caused a lot of discussion and I know for a fact that we played a big part in some people from the punk and animal rights scene refusing to go." At the same time, those punks who decided not to do their military service did not exclude those who did.

Ishay was investigated by the police in the late 1990s when he wrote an article for his fanzine advising young punks on how to dodge the draft. He, like the rest of Useless ID, did not serve in the army but did not have to serve jail time – as he might have had to today. "I did what I had to do in order to escape it in a legal manner, which was total refusal and a lot of convincing that this is ideal for both sides."

Nekhei Na'atza split in 1997 but Useless ID's career was just beginning. That year they released their first full album, *Dead's Not Punk*, on their own label, Falafel Records, and then in 1999 came their second, *Get in the Pita Bread Pit*. Then the frontman of US punk rock band The Ataris, Kris Roe, invited the band to record a split EP featuring nine of his songs and seven by Useless ID. One of the songs, 'Too Bad You Don't Get It', was featured on Fat Wreck Chords' *Short Music for Short People* (a compilation that saw 101 bands perform songs less than 30 seconds long). The exposure led to Useless ID being signed by Kung Fu Records, the US label started by American punk band The Vandals.

But as their career was beginning to pick up, the situation in Israel was deteriorating. On 25 February 1994, Baruch Goldstein massacred 29 worshippers at Hebron's Mosque of Abraham. After Rabin's death, right-winger Benjamin Netanyahu won the Israeli leadership and began dismantling the peace that the late leader had forged. Bands like Useless ID and Nekhei Na'atza had fought hard against the tide of militarism in Israel, but by the end of the millennium the stage was set not for peace, but for war.

* * *

On the outskirts of Gaza City, tower blocks are riddled with shrapnel and smog hangs over the buildings like a storm cloud. On the roads, battered taxis jostle with trucks and occasional men on horseback and pockmarked buildings are emblazoned with graffiti, flags and posters of the *shaheed* – or martyrs – killed in the regular wars with Israel.

Unlike the West Bank, which has benefited from billions of dollars in investment and foreign aid money (flowing all too often into the pockets of well-connected Fatah officials and their friends), Gaza is largely undeveloped, desperately poor and home to some 2 million people packed into an area of just 365 square kilometres. In refugee camps such as al-Shati – known as Beach Camp – sprawling networks of collapsing houses are set around tiny alleys and dusty squares. Many of these refugees were driven out of the cities to the south and even from as far north as Tel Aviv in 1948: the kids who fly kites and play football on the hot tarmac and sandy wasteland are their children and grandchildren. Around 65 per cent of Gaza's population is under the age of 24 and 43 per cent are under the age of 14.

Gaza has become home to returning Palestinians from other Arab states too, many of whom fled in 1948 for countries such as Tunisia, Algeria and Syria. Ayman Mghamis moved to the Gaza Strip in 1996 from Tunisia, travelling through Egypt with his family to the border at Rafah. In the mid-1990s the crossing was still controlled by Israel, and so when Ayman arrived he was surprised to see burly Israeli soldiers searching their luggage and checking their papers. "I asked my Mom: 'Aren't we coming back to Palestine because it is liberated? Why are these soldiers speaking Hebrew and why are they holding their guns in our faces?' My Mom didn't answer me at the time. She said we'll talk about it later," he said.

It has become common to talk with nostalgia of the years prior to the Second Intifada, when Israelis could drive to Gaza City, Khan Younis and Rafah from Tel Aviv to shop, hang out on the beach or visit Palestinian hotels and resorts that lined the shore. But Gaza was a territory under occupation, and while hundreds of thousands of Palestinians would travel north to work on Israeli farms and in cities such as Ashkelon and Tel Aviv, they were subject to checkpoints, searches and interrogations. In the 40 years since Israel had captured Gaza during the Six Day War, Israeli settlers had built up houses in communities that resembled Los Angeles rather than Palestine. The majority of Arabs in Gaza, meanwhile, lived in shabby apartment blocks and refugee camps. With the outbreak of the intifada, Gaza – like the West Bank – became a war zone.

It wasn't just conflicts with the Israelis that defined Ayman's early years in Palestine, but also with other Palestinians. Gaza was already a hugely overcrowded place and the Palestinians whose families had lived there since before 1948 resented the new arrivals, regardless of the fact that their heritage was the same. "I was always telling myself that this is my country as it is theirs and I had the right to live here as they have," he said.

Ayman was 16 when the Second Intifada began and the bloodshed led to two realisations that would go on to define his life: first, that he didn't want to die; and second, that he wanted to do something to help his people and his country.

It was during the conflict that he first heard the music of DAM, the Palestinian hip hop crew from Lod, in Israel. He had always been a fan of western hip hop as well as country music, rock and R&B, but saw in DAM's political message an opportunity to articulate the Palestinian struggle in a form that did not involve violence and was unlikely – or at least less likely – to get him killed. He began rapping in Arabic with friends and formed the Gaza Strip's first hip hop crew, Palestinian Rapperz.

In 2005, Israel dismantled its settlements in Gaza and withdrew its military from the Strip. Palestinian elections followed and when Hamas, the Islamist movement, won in Gaza and the West Bank city of Hebron, its rival Fatah refused to accept the result. Fatah and Hamas fought a quick but bloody civil war during 2006 that resulted in the latter taking control of Gaza and the former the West Bank. Israel responded by shutting the border with Gaza, refusing to deal with a group that openly calls for its destruction.

Along with Hamas' rule came numerous other changes in Gaza: the banning of alcohol and the widespread wearing of hijabs, which – while not the law – have been worn by the majority of women in the Strip ever since. It was more difficult for musicians too. "It wasn't easy to start rap music in Gaza because it's a closed community and considered a conservative one. We faced all kinds of criticism at the beginning. But we continued because we believe in music as a positive weapon that we can reach the universe through," he said.

Ayman's message would be tested in late 2008 when Israel launched its first war on the Strip: Operation Cast Lead. During a bombing raid in Gaza City, Ayman's house was destroyed and his father was killed. It was 16 January, his birthday.

In the days following his death, Ayman sat down and wrote a song, 'Madinati' ('My City'), in which he recounted in harrowing detail his last minutes with his father as he died.

His last words followed by his last breath
Asking my mother to take care of her children
It was me who wiped her tears
I gathered my wounds of sadness and enshrouded
    them
Then I buried them in my heart.

The song was recorded with DAM's Tamer Nafar and another Palestinian rapper, Shadia Mansour, who lives in London. Even before he wrote the song, Ayman had already come to international attention, featuring in numerous documentaries and hip hop compilations and inspiring reams of newspaper and magazine articles.

In the years since, Ayman has performed whenever he has been able to get out of Gaza, including in Egypt, Dubai, Ireland and the US. But since his father's death, his priorities have changed. "At the beginning I wanted to fight with words and invest my talent. I used to have dreams and he always supported me but now I'm fighting alone and it's not working. Every time I feel that I make progress something else happens and takes me ten steps backwards," he said.

Gaza, too, has slipped backwards. In the summer of 2014, war between Hamas and Israel broke out, and as rockets were fired at Israeli cities, Israeli shells pounded Gaza. Over 2,100 Palestinians were killed, with seven in ten of them civilians according to the United Nations.

During the war, Ayman worked as an interpreter for dozens of the journalists who descended on the Strip during the 50-day conflict and the bloodshed and destruction took him back to 2009 and his father's death. "I was in the field helping with injuries whenever I could," he said.

His memories of the conflict have found their way into his new material, as has the increasing frustration on the part of Gazans, who see their leaders – whether Fatah or Hamas – as having brought them only corruption and conflict since 2006. Ayman now worries about the life of his daughter and his nephew, growing up in Gaza, sealed off from the world and with the threat of another war with Israel close. Even supporters of Hamas have had enough of the conflict. "They want peace but they can't say it out loud because they are afraid of their leaders. One day they will have the balls to speak up."

But the effect of the war was felt not only in terms of the death toll. For the first time, shrapnel was landing in Tel Aviv and other cities further north, including Jerusalem. Even if most of the rockets were first blasted out of the sky by Israel's high-tech missile defence system, the Iron Dome, the air raid sirens and explosions that shook windows and had residents cowering in stairwells and bomb shelters became a reality in Tel Aviv and Jerusalem in a way that they had not been since the intifada. In the West Bank, masked youths fought pitched battles with Israeli soldiers on the streets of Bethlehem, Ramallah, Nablus and Jenin – many young Palestinians were killed, and the cycle of violence continued.

In Tel Aviv, always known as 'the bubble' because of its liberal, left-wing politics and its freewheeling, beach bum, partying lifestyle, there was a sharp change in attitudes: people who had once condemned the occupation and had been sympathetic to the plight of the Palestinians suddenly became supportive of the Netanyahu government and the onslaught in Gaza. For Israelis in their late teens and early twenties who had grown up in the era of the separation wall, Sharon and Netanyahu, the wars in Gaza and the intifada, all they knew of young Palestinians was violence. For Palestinians in the West Bank and Gaza, all they knew of Israelis had come from humiliation at checkpoints or from behind the barrels of guns. The wanton bloodshed in Gaza in 2014 was seen by many as the final nail in the coffin of co-existence.

* * *

System Ali was founded in the southern neighbourhood of Ajami, close to Jaffa, in a disused bomb shelter that had been given to the group by the Tel Aviv municipality. A collective, its 11 members created music in four languages – Hebrew, Arabic, Russian and English – and fused hip hop with jazz, rock and electronic music, with violins and accordions alongside guitars, drums and vocals. Neta Weiner, a rapper and accordion player with the collective, said that in the ten years since System Ali was founded, the band is yet to have a crowd member who can speak all four languages.

System Ali was originally formed of five Israelis, who opted to do NGO work instead of serving in the military. They worked in schools throughout Jaffa doing everything from conducting music workshops to teaching martial arts. The areas they worked in tended to be poor, giving them an insight into the challenges of integration in Israel in the mid-2000s. "One of the schools we went to, 90 per cent of the students were Palestinians from Jaffa or newcomers from the former Soviet Union and it was written on the blackboard of every classroom you are not allowed to speak Russian or Arabic in class," Neta said.

When the five moved to the bomb shelter – which they named Beit System Ali – they drew on these experiences for their music. Divisions and disparity between Palestinians and Israelis, between Mizrahi and Ashkenazi Jews, between older immigrant communities from Russia and newer ones from Ethiopia – all had an impact on what would become their sound. "These things were fuel for System Ali. They were the experiences that shaped us both as a band and as an NGO," Neta said.

The regular jam sessions that System Ali held at the bomb shelter in Ajami brought in many musicians, including rappers Muhammed Mugrabi and Amneh Jarushi, percussionist Luna Abu-Nasar and violinist Liba Neeman. Another rapper, Enver Seitibragimov, was from a Russian background and rapped in his native language, alongside choruses in Hebrew and Arabic. It was exciting, Neta said, but daunting too: "Musicians and poets came by to speak on the microphone for the first time. People spoke in the languages they could express themselves best in. It was beautiful and inspiring – but also very hard."

Every once in a while, the conflicts over music would get out of hand – even resulting in band members coming to blows. When Muhammed Mugrabi wrote the lyrics for a song, 'Insa', which means 'forget' in Arabic, about what he had to endure as a Palestinian living in Israel, Enver wrote a verse in response about the similar emotions he felt coming as an immigrant from Russia. Muhammed felt that the plight of Palestinians could not be compared with that of Russians and the two began arguing – then they began fighting. "It just exploded. But after it became a song. We are proud of it; we all have a part in the discussion," Neta said.

The conflict reflects the fact that, in bringing together people of very different heritage, System Ali are not trying to mould a new identity but explore how several different identities can exist at the same time in the same country. "The last thing you want to do is say that this is a melting pot and we want to mould something new. Everyone has to bring themselves 100 per cent and sometimes it creates tension. Now we've been working together for ten years and it is actually like a small family. But you have fights inside a family," he said.

Soon after the band's formation, System Ali were shaken by the outbreak of the 2008–09 war in Gaza. Palestinian members of the band had family in Gaza while Israelis had friends and family fighting for the Israel Defense Forces. Suddenly the arguments were not about legitimacy or discrimination, but about a conflict that was taking place just a few dozen miles to the south. "The discussions about it were very real. People were in a situation of madness when people are getting murdered and people are afraid for their families. But you have compassion and love for people who are like brothers – or like siblings – to you," Neta said.

> I wasn't sure we were going to make it; I wasn't
> sure System Ali would survive those few weeks in
> 2009 – there were times that I thought it was not
> possible. We had a lot of fight and tears during that
> time. But I think in certain ways System Ali was
> born for a second time.

Neta was born in a kibbutz in central Israel that had been built by his grandparents before moving to a small village further north, near the border with Syria and Lebanon. From the beginning, he grew up in a society that was strictly separated between Arabs and Jews. But when he was 14 he started visiting the closest Arab village to his town and hanging out with young Palestinians of a similar age. He visited Jaffa for the first time, which was then – as now – a mixed neighbourhood where Palestinians and Israelis lived side by side. His parents sent him to boarding school in Jerusalem, where he studied alongside both Jewish and Arab students, but after graduating he ended up back in Jaffa and began composing music that drew from his life there. "I tried to make it a reflection of what I could find in Jaffa personally. It is not my place; I still feel like a stranger in it," he said. Jaffa's rich history as a thriving port under the Romans, Ottomans and then under the British Mandate of Palestine had always made it a multicultural city, even if thousands of Palestinians had been driven south to Gaza or overseas during the foundation of Israel in 1948. "The richness, culturally speaking, is still here and it is for a good reason that System Ali are here," Neta said.

Neta disputes that System Ali are necessarily a left-wing band, or that they are pro-Palestinian.

It is not what you would expect. Even the Jewish
members are very varied: there are religious
people, people who call themselves secular. It
is a really mixed group. In terms of what you
would characterise as left-wing or right-wing, it
is confusing and this is the way we like it. These
categories, they don't serve us in any way.

The band's first show was to highlight the struggle
for housing rights in rapidly gentrifying Jaffa, where poor
residents of all backgrounds were being pushed out by high
rents and development. In response to the benefit gig, the
Tel Aviv municipality closed down the bomb shelter that
was their base.

System Ali were lucky enough to find a new space in
nearby Bat Yam, and they have since converted it into a
recording studio and performance space. They are currently
working with 150 artists from a variety of backgrounds,
from Palestinians to Eritrean and Sudanese refugees,
thousands of whom have crossed the Sinai into Israel over
the past decade and have settled in the ramshackle districts
of south Tel Aviv. Until he was deported, one of System
Ali's founding members was a rapper from Eritrea.

The bonds that have been formed were such that when
yet another war broke out in Gaza in 2014, System Ali
fared better than they had in 2009. "We couldn't believe it

was happening again, but we were a bit older and we had experienced the situation already so we could find a place for our rage in each other. It helped, a lot," Neta said.

The band wrote a group of songs titled *Let My People Go* that they are now recording as a follow-up to their self-titled first album. It is an effort, Neta said, to encourage people to talk about conflict in Israel and Palestine and within Israeli and Palestinian society. "One of the things that drove us crazy in 2009 was the silence. Everything was hell but you couldn't say anything, you weren't allowed to, you weren't expected to," he said.

A situation like the intifada brings forward a lot of violence but also a lot of voices. I think these are periods of truth, because even though there are the most awful opinions, at least things are open and people speak out. You can get a picture of how bad things are in terms of rage.

* * *

In the second half of the 2000s, Useless ID's focus began to shift back to Israel, and in 2009 they released their first album in Hebrew alongside a hip hop reggae artist, Muki. They supported No Use for a Name in Tel Aviv and then toured the country with a series of headline shows. "I guess we did try to focus more on doing things in Israel at certain points, but things like the Hebrew album ... I don't know. I think that maybe we were hoping to get some more recognition in our home, and looking back now, it means very little to me, personally," Ishay said.

Useless ID signed to Fat Wreck Chords in 2012 and Ishay's younger brother, Gideon, joined the band. In April 2016 they released *State is Burning*, their eighth full-length album. Despite songs such as 'Borrowed Time', which lashes out at greedy, lying politicians, or the title track, which is a direct snub to the acceptance that they once sought in Israel, Ishay disputes that Useless ID are a political band. "I don't describe any band as a political band. For me it's like: 'Is that a good band? A bad band? A fast band? A slow band?' And in 2016 I would describe Useless ID as a good, fast band," he said. Of the scene they helped to establish back in the 1990s, Ishay is pessimistic:

Kids leave the scene at the age of 18 because they have to go to the army, and the cycle goes on and on. It's a little sad to say this but the only major change in the scene, 20 years later, is the internet. Kids can order records and shirts and get in touch with other people in a different, more intense way. We used to send regular mail and trade fanzines and tapes and now everything is done in a completely different way, and, sadly, that's the biggest change that I see.

In 2000, Federico flew to Sweden to marry his girlfriend, Jenny. They returned to Israel but a few days later the intifada broke out. Although Federico tried to remain politically active, he struggled to come to terms with what was happening to his adopted country. "I think that for both Jenny and me, the political situation turned hopeless and it had a big impact on our feelings towards Israel," he said. In late 2005, he left Israel and moved to Falun, in Sweden, to train as a teacher. After a few years the couple moved to Stockholm, where they live now with their two sons.

Federico is nostalgic about the years 1992 to 1996, when the scene in Tel Aviv, Haifa and Jerusalem was tight-knit and the political situation in Israel was less intolerant than it is today. "I'm neither politically active nor doing something scene-wise besides going to the odd show every now and then. I really miss making music and, of course, the friends who were involved in the 1990s Israeli punk scene," he said.

He sees Nekhei Na'atza as having achieved what they set out to do – creating a genuine underground scene in Israel – and his only regret is that the band was so lax about recording their music professionally, to the extent that very little of it has survived to the present day. "We were naïve and ignorant about the more technical aspects of music and that side of being in a band didn't, unfortunately, match our enthusiasm for trying to change things. We should have rehearsed more as well," he said. "But one of our main goals was to start a DIY punk scene in Israel and we, along with several others, definitely achieved that."

Israel, however, has changed since the mid-1990s and he does not see many of the stances that Nekhei Na'atza took back then being accepted today: "I would say that the mood in early to mid-1990s Israel wasn't as xenophobic and intolerant as it seems to be now."

* * *

In Gaza, Ayman Mghamis is increasingly restless, even if in the time he has been into hip hop more than 30 rappers have emerged in the Strip. He is reluctant to say that he is fed up with fighting, but life has had to take a front seat. The people he rapped with when he started out have mostly left Palestine in search of a better life. He has a mother and sister to look out for, as well as a daughter and another baby on the way. "They are my family and I can't be selfish in my thinking and leave all of them behind," he said.

Instead, he is hoping to pass on the hip hop mantle to a new generation of Gazan rappers, to find young voices who can stand alongside him and continue to sing about the struggle. "I can say that I have succeeded somehow directly and indirectly to create a phenomenon in Gaza and now rap is becoming more popular despite all the efforts of the government to shut our mouths," he said. Ayman recently led a Swedish-funded project that taught rappers and musicians to record their material as well as music theory.

They have 21 individuals enrolled on the programme and the waiting list is far longer.

He sees talent and drive amongst young rappers in Gaza: he can only imagine what could be achieved if the checkpoints were dismantled and its people were free. "We don't have the space to breathe and still we refuse to give up and still our voices are heard," he said. "With a little more space, imagine what we could achieve."

Ashmedi became a Dutch citizen, and although he regularly returns to Jerusalem on vacation, his life and work are now in Europe, where Melechesh are an internationally renowned band. Max Cavalera, the Sepultura founder, recently guested on a Melechesh song, 'Lost Tribes'. Their growing following in Israel, where they were once shunned, has even stretched to the West Bank: Melechesh was recently *This Week in Palestine*'s Artist of the Month, the first time that a heavy metal band has ever been profiled in the Palestinian press. From Egypt to Lebanon to Saudi Arabia, metal bands cite Melechesh as an influence, and at international shows and signing sessions Lebanese fans will be queuing next to Israelis. But unlike other bands – such as Orphaned Land – who have made co-existence very much part of their narrative, Ashmedi has little interest in playing that role: "We don't get paid to sing about peace," he said.

DAM remain the undisputed kings of Middle East hip hop and Tamer has written and starred in his first film, the critically acclaimed *Junction 48*. Directed by Udi Aloni, it tells the story of a young Palestinian, Kareem, from Lod trying to make it as a rapper.

Tamer has worked with rappers from other parts of the Middle East, including MC Amin in Egypt, and with Israel-based groups such as System Ali. Ironically, he also finds himself having to listen to a lot of Hebrew hip hop because his sons, aged three and seven, like it. "It's fun. It makes them dance and it makes them happy. I am OK with that," he said.

As for his writing, he has found himself looking to Leonard Cohen and Bob Dylan as much as to the US hip hop that was once his main inspiration. He has been working on a song about his late father, an early supporter of the band even when they were nobodies playing to a handful of people in a sweaty club in Tel Aviv. He was a devout Muslim who was confined to a wheelchair after a car accident, and Tamer remembered that he and his brother would have to carry him up the stairs when he came to shows. "He was very proud of what we were trying to establish. He saw the fame – he saw us when there were only three people in the concert, and before he died he saw concerts with thousands of people," he said.

Behind this wish to diversify, to sing about love and loss, to make films and to experiment with new genres, is Tamer's desire to be more than the standard-bearer for the Palestinian cause. He resents the fact that the struggle against Israeli occupation alone has defined them. He resents the fact that, in the West, DAM are only seen as a vehicle for politics. He resents that, were it not for Israel's treatment of Arabs and the occupation and the global solidarity movement, many of those who champion DAM and their music would lose interest. Above all, he is sick of Palestinians being defined only by their relationship to Israel. "We have people dying from the army and massacres – but we also have people dying from cancer and fucking car accidents. It is wrong for the liberals who defend us to have one thought about us. We are different," he said.

Tamer believes that the tendency on the part of Palestine's supporters to see it as a homogeneous block of people rather than individuals has had an impact on the new generation of rappers who were inspired by DAM's music.

> I sit backstage with ten other rappers and we talk. We talk about Palestine, of course. We talk about Gaza, whatever is happening in the news. But then we talk about the new Narcos that is coming up on Netflix. We talk about sex and we show each other photos of beautiful girls. We talk about alcohol and we drink. And then they go on stage and it's like all their songs are "Free Free Palestine, Free Free Palestine". I appreciate that a lot of people here are trying to help the cause, but I don't like the fact that they don't believe that they can exist without the occupation – it is like Stockholm syndrome. Like

we need the Israelis so we can continue doing songs
and we need the occupation to create.

At the heart of Tamer's film, *Junction 48*, is his latest song, 'Ya Reit' ('If Only'), the first love song he has ever written. It tells of how he can sing about anything, about the occupation, the wall, the plight of Palestinians growing up in Lod or in Gaza, but he can't sing about love.

When we speak, he is frustrated by the questions about Israel, about Palestine, about conservatism and conflict. He wonders why nobody ever asks him about the other songs, the songs about sex, or smoking shisha. He wonders whether he – and DAM – will ever be more than a vessel for opposition to Israel. "It started a long time ago. It's like when your Dad has a successful business and you want to do something else, but your Dad keeps pushing you not to do something else," he says. "Now I am trying to do something without the message but people still want me to deliver the fucking message."

Tamer knows he has a responsibility, with his profile and his reach, to try to change things for Palestinians. He remains a committed activist. But in his music he is seeking something more, he is seeking freedom. "I would like to believe that even if the Middle East was a better place and there was no occupation," he said, "I would like to believe that I would still be relevant."

CHAPTER 6
SYRIA

There was a point, adrift in the open sea, the engine gone, the rubber boat half deflated, the screams of men and women all around him, when Adel Saflou found himself singing. They were lost in the Mediterranean and many of the 50 men, women and children who clung to the rails of the dinghy were by now hysterical. Adel had managed to get his phone working and dialled the number he had been given by the people smugglers in Izmir, Turkey, to reach the Greek coastguard. Now he was on hold and there was music was playing over the line as he waited to be connected – and then he realised what he was listening to: it was 'Somewhere Over the Rainbow'. "I was thinking: 'Oh my God, am I really listening to this?' And everyone else is screaming, everyone is screaming and crying, and I am looking at them I am humming along," he said.

Eight hours earlier, Adel had packed into a van with two of his cousins, their children and some neighbours from his home city of Idlib, in northern Syria, as well as dozens of strangers. Adel and his cousins had paid $1,200 per person to cross from Izmir to Samos in Greece and the Turkish-Syrian smuggling gang had promised the family that their boat would have no more than 30 people on board, but it was clear when they arrived that they had been lying. He had toyed with the idea of buying his own boat – which went for around $3,000 in Turkey – and making the crossing himself, but considered it too dangerous. Adel had heard that the smugglers would often pursue boats that tried to cross alone and puncture them when they were at sea. In the summer of 2015, Izmir was full of Syrians waiting to make the crossing and word travelled fast between friends and family about the ruthless tactics of the smuggling gangs. "They are smugglers – they're criminals – in the end. They don't want you to be happy, they just want money," he said.

On the beach, Adel helped some of the younger kids put on their life jackets. It was a warm night but the water was cold as they waded to the boats. Adel had all of his cash wrapped in plastic and taped to his chest. They packed in, families tried to sit as close together as possible, but children and heavier passengers were shifted around to maintain the balance of the boat. The last person to board looked bemused as one of the smugglers handed him the tiller of the small outboard motor and then pointed out to sea, towards a twinkling crescent of lights in the distance. It was Greece. "*Yallah*: go – that way," he said, and pushed the craft into the swell. "No one knew what they were doing," Adel recalled.

And why would they? Like Adel, many of the refugees packed into the boat were middle-class Syrians from metropolitan cities like Idlib, hundreds of miles from the coast. An experienced skipper would struggle to pilot a heavily overloaded dinghy with no lights, no radio and no navigation system across 50 miles of open sea. Prior to the outbreak of Syria's bloody civil war, many of Adel's fellow passengers had regular lives – jobs, homes, families and friends – and yet they had found themselves chased out of their cities into refugee camps in countries that didn't want them. In Istanbul and Izmir they had had to negotiate safe passage for a fair price from criminal gangs. Now here they were, together, on the open sea in a final bid for sanctuary in Europe.

The sea was manageable in the first half an hour of the crossing, but as they left the safety of the Turkish coast for deeper waters the current and wind whipped up huge waves all around them. As water sloshed over the edges of the dinghy – already low in the water – people jammed themselves together to get away from it. Panic came quickly. "People were standing up. A lot of people were screaming, others were telling them to calm down. Then people started getting agitated and more water started coming in the boat," he said.

Adel quickly realised that they were sinking and he and his cousins considered diving into the water and swimming, but the swell made it impossible. At one point, a man leapt over the side but quickly faltered in the cold water and the others were able to drag him back to safety.

In the centre of the boat, where families were now crammed together, people were already screaming at each other: "People were shouting 'Don't touch my sister!' and 'I'm going to kill you' and 'I'm going to slice your throat'," Adel said. Then the designated pilot lost his temper and began wrenching furiously at the tiller. The engine came loose and dropped into the ink-black water. The boat was adrift. Their only hope now was rescue.

*　*　*

Adel had already left Syria when rebels stormed Idlib in 2015 and converted the house in which he grew up into a makeshift military base. His family had fled hours earlier after three years of living on the front line between the forces of Bashar al-Assad and the al-Qaeda-linked Jabhat al-Nusra rebels, and they eventually made it to a refugee camp in southern Turkey.

Adel was already in Beirut, where he had moved to in the early days of the war, and heard the story later from neighbours. "The rebels went into my room and it was painted dark red, all over. I had a big sword and two guitars and a painting of a pentagram. It looked really ritualistic," Adel said. On his shelves were books about heavy metal and CDs of bands from Europe and the US, while his walls were covered in pictures of shows he had attended in Syria and further afield. His pentagram, which he had drawn in black candle wax, must have been a shock to the pious Sunni rebels waging holy war in Syria: "They saw my picture and they said: 'We want this guy – he's a devil worshipper.' And now they have my name, I guess," he said. "I don't care. I am never going back there."

Growing up in Idlib it was difficult not to be swept up in the tide of anger towards Bashar al-Assad's Alawite regime, which had long discriminated against Syrian Sunnis like Adel's family. He had grown up in a household that had witnessed Assad's father, Hafez, brutally put down a Sunni uprising in the 1980s and raze the city of Hama to the ground, killing over 20,000 people.

While Assad's Baathist movement was ostensibly secular, in reality Hafez and Assad's Alawite sect dominated positions of power and influence in pre-war Syria while his secret police kept the Sunnis in check. Even if Adel was not political – let alone sectarian – growing up, a hatred of the Syrian government was in his blood. He remembered clearly when he was eight or nine how he and his friends would go down to the main square in Idlib and spit at the statue of Hafez.

Adel was raised to be religious. He prayed often and his mother and father were devout Muslims. But he also loved video games. In his early teens he bought 'Need for

Speed', the soundtrack of which included music by Avenged Sevenfold and Bullet For My Valentine, and as he raced cars through digital renderings of American cities or lush mountains he would look forward to the songs by these popular mid-2000s bands, then at the forefront of a popular genre known as metal-core.

On Syrian TV he first heard Foo Fighters, Gorillaz and Avril Lavigne, who were then topping the international charts, and after school he would go home, turn on the television and jump on his bed to the music. Then, in his early teens, he was hanging out at his cousins' house in the nearby town of Mera'a when he first heard Opeth, and his life changed forever. "I got hooked," he said. "It put a spell on me."

Adel managed to get hold of a classical guitar and began practising playing heavy metal songs at home. He migrated from Avril Lavigne to Metallica and Godsmack, and gradually got hold of heavy metal garb – spiked and studded bracelets, black band T-shirts – from the very few shops that sold them. He began going out with '666' and pentagrams drawn on felt tip pen on his hands. He got his first piercing.

But his new passion for heavy music, alternative fashion and the symbols of the occult did not go down well in conservative Idlib: "Metal was still really frowned on then. My family said it was devil worshipping. They all made a big deal out of it. It gave me a headache," he said.

In 2010, Adel moved to Aleppo with his mother, who took a teaching job in the city. Aleppo was then a relatively liberal financial centre of around 2 million people. It was also, alongside Damascus and Homs, one of three hubs for the Syrian metal scene. Adel quickly fell in with the crowd there and formed a band with scene stalwart, Bashar Haroun, who ran U-Ground Studios, then the main hangout for Aleppo's metallers. "It was easy to form bands in the studio. You were just sitting there and people would be like: 'Hey, you want to join a band?' Everyone played something and the best players always knew who to pick," he said.

His band, Orchid, rehearsed only three times before their first gig in 2010, and Adel only remembers now that it was at a bar called Cheers in Aleppo and that around 70 people turned up. After that, they continued to organise shows and the crowds grew. "For two years it was amazing and the studio was like a home. I spent most of my time there playing music. We'd smoke and talk and laugh and we'd get drunk," he said.

It's hard to believe it now, but most of those who lived through the protests that began in Syria during 2011 describe them as an overwhelmingly positive movement. It brought both Sunni and Shia Syrians onto the streets to protest against a shared enemy: Bashar al-Assad and his cronies. Many of Syria's richest and most powerful people came from within Bashar's own family. His brother, Maher, controlled the country's Republican Guard. His cousin, Rami Makhlouf, is Syria's richest man and perhaps the second most hated man in Syria (after Bashar). Syria was an ugly police state where a small cabal got rich as the rest of the population – Shia, Sunni, Kurdish or Christian – struggled to get by. The revolution may have begun in the Sunni majority cities of Homs and Hama, but within months the whole country was involved.

Assad had taken power in 2000 after his brother and Hafez al-Assad's heir-apparent, Bassel, was killed in a car crash. Bashar had been living a relatively normal life in London, working as an eye doctor and married to an English woman, Asma, an investment banker. That background persuaded many that the young Assad would finally put Syria on a path to democracy. But it wasn't to be; by 2010, Syria was every bit the police state it was under Hafez, and Bashar as ruthless a dictator as his father. When the Arab revolutions began in Tunisia 2010 and in Egypt and Libya at the beginning of 2011, it was only natural that Syria was next.

On 15 March, crowds took to the streets of the southern city of Dera'a to call for the release of political prisoners and an end to corruption. As the protests grew to other Syrian cities, including Hama and Homs, Assad lifted a 48-year-old state of emergency and released dozens of political prisoners. He also made concessions to Syria's Islamists by lifting the country's ban on women wearing the full face veil – the niqab – and closing the country's only casino. But it wasn't enough.

From the earliest days of the conflict, Assad also responded to the protests with violence. Tens of thousands of opposition activists were rounded up in door-to-door searches in cities such as Idlib, and both Dera'a and Hama were put under siege by government tanks and artillery. At the end of July 2011, Syrian defectors founded the Free Syrian Army (FSA) and by December Damascus had seen its first suicide bombing, with 44 people killed. The Syrian regime began the bombardment of Homs and Hama that continued into 2012, and with every report of mass civilian casualties, the protest movement grew.

In Aleppo, Adel, who finished school in the summer of 2012, saw the escalation first-hand when he returned to Idlib, which had been an early conquest of anti-Assad rebels before being seized by the government in April. The city was a battleground. Syrian regime thugs were going door to door seeking out rebel sympathisers, which often simply translated as anyone young, Sunni and male, with rebels camped on the outskirts. "It was terrible there," Adel said.

From a practical perspective, Adel wanted to study English, but even in peacetime the universities in Idlib did not offer it. Likewise, his musical ambitions were hardly going to be satisfied in a city already torn apart by a spiralling conflict. But there was a religious dimension too. Syria's conflict had not yet taken on the horrific sectarian dimension that it had by 2013. Syria-sponsored Shia militant group Hezbollah had not yet entered the war on the side of Assad, ISIS was still a ragtag group of Sunni militants hiding out in Syria's eastern deserts. Saudi Arabia, Qatar and Turkey had not yet started funding Sunni groups such as Jabhat al-Nusra, and the FSA was still a credible – and multi-denominational – political force.

But it was clear to Adel even in 2012 that the conflict was about to get much worse. It was not safe for a guy who walked around with piercings and '666' written on his hands to remain in Syria. "For me as a musician, it was not a good idea to stay in Syria – anything could happen. I didn't want to waste my life or test my luck."

Like an increasing number of refugees from Syria, Adel packed his bags and headed across the border to Lebanon.

* * *

Yasser Jamous got hold of his first hip hop album in 2001 by accident. His uncle, a passionate break dancer, had sent him to a music shop near his home in Yarmouk, outside Damascus, to pick up a mix tape. Yasser headed to his local music store with a blank cassette and a list of the tracks that his uncle wanted, but when the owner had finished copying the songs he said there was still 30 minutes spare. The owner started talking about an American rapper who had just released a new album, and said he would put as much as he could of it on the end of the tape. That was how a teenage Palestinian refugee in the Middle East's biggest refugee camp discovered Eminem: "I liked his music," Yasser said. "It was commercial but it was my doorway into hip hop."

From there, Yasser began looking into the roots of Eminem's music: Tupac, Biggie Smalls and N.W.A. "It was crazy. It just had this amazing energy," he said. Yasser began writing out the lyrics to his favourite songs and looking into the meanings, and found that the life that rappers like Eminem, Tupac, Biggie and Ice Cube were describing in Detroit, Brooklyn and Los Angeles had parallels with his own as a refugee, growing up in a large and impoverished area of Syria where violence was never far away. "I started to feel the lyrics and the idea of resisting. I felt that there were real issues inside this music," he said.

Prior to the war, Yarmouk was home to around 160,000 people, most of them Palestinian refugees who were forced from their homes after the foundation of Israel in 1948. Unlike the refugee camps of Turkey or Jordan today, Yarmouk was not a sprawling tent city but a shabby suburb of Damascus that had developed over 60 years, with shops, restaurants, roads and businesses. Like the camps of the Palestinian West Bank, Yarmouk was practically a functioning city – but unlike the West Bank, Palestinians living there were able to travel into Damascus or elsewhere in the country relatively freely. Like Palestinian camps in Jordan and Lebanon, various districts of Yarmouk were effectively governed and operated by factions of Palestinian militias. As a result, while many Yarmouk residents were born in Syria, Palestinian identity was strong in the camp. It was Palestinian flags and the colours of the militias – red for the Marxist PFLP (Popular Front for the Liberation of Palestine), green for the Islamist Hamas and yellow for Yasser Arafat's Fatah – that flew over the houses, rather than Syrian flags.

But Palestinian Yarmouk residents were not Syrian citizens – they were guests – and infrastructure, sanitation and resources in the camp were far inferior to those in Damascus or other Syrian cities. Just as the music of Eminem documented the US rapper's experience of growing up on the wrong side of Detroit's Eight Mile Road – where poverty was rife and prospects for young people slim – so Yasser's early lyrics documented not only his identity as a Palestinian but the day-to-day lives of young people in the camp.

Yasser and his brother, Mohammed, began to write in English before shifting to Arabic, and until 2006 they kept themselves to themselves, recording a couple of songs through a microphone attached to their family computer. They were convinced that they were the only people in the Middle East rapping in Arabic. But one day they headed to an internet cafe and Googled 'Arabic hip hop' and came across a Palestinian site with some songs by DAM. They were surprised to also find another site dedicated to Syrian hip hop and featuring bands from Homs and Aleppo and at least two from Damascus. "It was a shock," Yasser recalled. "My brother messaged one of the guys and said we liked his song and if he was in Damascus we should meet. He replied: 'OK, where do you live?' and we said Yarmouk and he said: 'What the fuck? I am in Yarmouk too.'"

That rapper, Muhammed Jawad, introduced Yasser and Mohammed to a fourth musician, Ahmad Razouk, an Algerian, and when the four met in Yarmouk they decided to work together. They tossed around a few names, but couldn't agree. It dawned on them that, of the group, two were Palestinian, one was Syrian and the other was Algerian, so at least three-quarters of the band were refugees. That was when they decided on Refugees of Rap. The name was to take on a new meaning a decade later when the group were forced to flee Syria, but even at a relatively peaceful time they thought that the word 'refugee' was fitting. "We thought all of us were refugees to rap music. We take rap music as a place to be free and write our lyrics, to find asylum. It was not political, it was more for us, as teenagers, to be released," Yasser said.

The first song Yasser and Mohammed had recorded as a pair was a love song and their second was about hanging out in their neighbourhood, but their first song as a band was different: "It was about us and rap and what it meant to us. It said: 'Forget the TV, we are the new TV. We will tell you the truth.' It was a teenage rebel song," Yasser said.

As Facebook and YouTube were blocked in Syria, the only way to publish songs was on the music-sharing site Myspace and the Syrian hip hop site, which was administered by another Syrian rapper called Mohammed Abu Hajjar. They contacted Abu Hajjar and when he put it up positive comments quickly began to pour in.

They also had more elaborate ways of sharing music, such as with Bluetooth between mobile phones in the streets of Yarmouk. At a time when very few computers in the refugee camp were connected to Wi-Fi, Bluetooth sharing made Refugees of Rap 'go viral':

> The way was to send it to a friend who sent it to a
> friend and so on. But after a week we started to hear
> our song in the street. We'd be walking along and
> we'd hear our song being played in a car and I was
> like – this is me! But nobody knew who we were.

The song grew in popularity with young Palestinians and Syrians in Yarmouk but the older generation was less receptive. Palestinians had long valued their traditional music, and in particular songs that spoke of their exile and their dream of return to Palestine, but rap was seen as an alien genre.

In Palestine, DAM had managed to achieve mainstream success amongst Palestinians because of their political message, and the same was true for Refugees of Rap. Their next song, 'Palestine and the Decision', was a direct attack on Arab states that had failed to support the Palestinian people and push for their homeland. It accused Arab nations, including Syria, of abandoning millions of Palestinians to a life of exile. It was an angry, upbeat and aggressive anthem that was far from the maudlinism of traditional Palestinian music. "It was a hit," said Yasser. "We counted and between Myspace and ReverbNation it had around 200,000 downloads in the first two months and eventually hit 500,000."

The band was contacted by rappers from Palestine who wanted to upload their song to a new hip hop site, Palrap. This allowed them to contact other artists from across the Middle East and put their first album together, the self-titled *Refugees of Rap*. They recorded one song at home and four more in a local studio, which was a huge expense. "We didn't have any income and our parents were not in a good situation financially. We suffered to get the money to go and record – sometimes we would have everything prepared but we didn't have the money for transport. We had the money to record but not to get to the studio," Yasser said.

Refugees of Rap also began performing at local clubs between DJ sets and by 2008 were doing so well that they would be asked to go on Syrian TV channels and perform concerts in Damascus. As their profile grew, the band struggled to get their increasingly political message across without falling foul of the authorities. Lyrically, Yasser and Mohammed began relying on metaphors and allusions to their politics rather than outright criticisms of the government. They also benefited from the fact that hip hop lyrics are spoken so quickly that many of the secret police officers at their gigs simply didn't understand them.

The band played in Cairo and in Beirut and at bigger and bigger shows in Damascus. When they did TV interviews, they would be asked to submit lyrics beforehand, but often, because they were seen as Palestinians talking about the Palestinian struggle rather than Syrians criticising the regime, they got away with more than a Syrian outfit would. The authorities were less tolerant of critics of the regime in Algeria, and they were banned at least once from performing on TV. "When we went to Syrian TV, they introduced us as Syrian, and on Arab TV as Palestinian. But we preferred not to be identified as a nationality. We were refugees and we wanted to be introduced as that," Yasser said.

In 2010 the band recorded another album, *Face to Face*, which included their first anti-regime song, 'Age of Silence'. They debated whether to release the song once the revolution began in 2011 but opted not to (it would not be made public until 2013). "We didn't release it fast enough. It was negative, I think, but we had been in danger – sharing the song in Syria was a crime," he said. But the band concluded that, with checkpoints throughout Damascus and their families living in Syria, they could not in good faith release a song that would endanger those they loved. "We decided we would find a way to get out and after we can do this," he said. Recording the song was difficult enough; Yasser remembered that the sound engineer was so nervous about its content that they had to attend the studio in the middle of the night.

While Homs and Hama were quickly captivated by the protests that began in 2011 in Dera'a and spread to the major cities, including Damascus, the revolution was less well received by many in Yarmouk. Many of the Palestinian factions that controlled the camp were loyal to Assad before the rebel movement, and those who had TVs had seen the chaos that was unfurling in Libya and Egypt.

Yarmouk was poverty-stricken and heavily reliant on aid, but, unlike in other Middle East countries, the Syrian regime permitted Palestinians to own property and to work. In the same way that many Palestinians had supported Saddam Hussein because of his ongoing belligerence towards Israel (compared with Egypt and Jordan, which both signed peace deals with the Jewish state), many Yarmouk residents saw

Assad as an ally in their struggle for a Palestinian state – not least given his open hostility towards Tel Aviv over Israel's occupation of the Golan Heights. As Yasser said:

> People were angry because of the actions of the regime but they were afraid to have the scenario of Libya. People were confused. In Yarmouk there was not really one opinion; there were many – even within one family.

What turned opinion in Yarmouk was the brutality with which Assad dealt with the protests in Dera'a, then besieged by the Syrian army. Yarmouk residents watched the footage of death and destruction with horror on YouTube and protests grew. As the rebels made inroads into the camp – which is a crucial front line for advances on Damascus – life became more and more dangerous. Government air strikes began in 2012 and Yarmouk residents took to the streets on 14 July in a mass protest: "I remember more than 80 per cent of the camp was in the street. The rest were on their balconies, throwing water to help people cool down. It was very hot but the whole camp was there," Yasser said.

The army opened fire and three Palestinians were killed. Then the FSA entered Yarmouk in 2012 and Yasser and Mohammed decided that enough was enough. Daily air strikes had destroyed swathes of the neighbourhood.

On the day they were due to leave, in December 2012, Yasser made a decision – he had to go to the studio, which was on the front line between Assad's forces and the FSA, and rescue what he could. "It was ten minutes from home but it was in a place where there were no civilians. I didn't tell my parents. I took my bicycle and I rode there," he said. As he walked in the door, he saw all of the equipment that the band had saved for months to buy and had spent years accumulating. He knew he couldn't carry the speakers, mixing desks and mics – they were too heavy – so he opened the monitors and removed the hard drives: "I would not let all that be lost. I took the disks and went back home. Six weeks later it was destroyed," he said.

Mohammed and Yasser called in a few favours and managed to secure French visas through a series of contacts, including an Italian rapper, a refugee charity, a European journalist and, finally, the French Consul in Lebanon. The pair made the two-hour drive to Beirut from Damascus and rocked up at the embassy with nothing more than backpacks and the Palestinian refugee IDs that they had been given in Syria. "I remember in the embassy, I asked the guy: 'How long will this take?' And he said sorry and that it would take a little more time. I said 'Like how many days?' and he said 'Like 30 minutes.'" He laughed. "We were like, fuck, what? I thought it would take two months." Within hours, they were at Beirut airport bound for France.

* * *

Oosthuizen is the kind of place where people go to die, Monzer Darwish said, peering through the net curtains at the silent street from the first-floor window of his flat. The tiny town is a prime destination for Dutch retirees and set in the low, green fields north of Amsterdam, just outside the tourist town of Edam – famous for its cheese.

Monzer and his wife, Lena, were two of the thousands of refugees who risked crossing the Mediterranean by boat in 2015. They then walked across Europe, bought fake passports in Greece and then flew to the Netherlands, where they claimed asylum. As is the policy in Holland, they were housed first in refugee centres and then allocated a flat in Oosthuizen. Here they spend their days watching TV and learning Dutch while Monzer, a filmmaker, worked on a documentary – *Syrian Metal Is War* – that he wrote and filmed in Syria between 2011 and 2013. Other than the TV, a couple of guitars and their cat, Monzer and Lena's flat was bare. When they crossed the Mediterranean they brought almost nothing with them.

Monzer grew up in Masyaf, near Hama, and remembers exactly when he discovered metal. He was in the seventh grade and was attending a computer competition. It was hot and he was wearing shorts, but when he arrived at the venue a security guard told him he would have to go home and change because there were young women also competing. Monzer refused. "I was really young and I didn't even know what he was talking about. I said I wouldn't change and I was kicked out of the competition," he said. Monzer went back to his room in tears and found a friend, who was also attending the event, listening to music through headphones. "He put the headphones on me and said: 'This will make you feel better.' And it did."

The song was 'Battery' by Metallica and the album, *Master of Puppets*, was Monzer's first heavy metal record. When he returned to Masyaf, he told his 70-year-old piano teacher what he had heard and was surprised when the old man dug out a cassette of Metallica's *Load* and gave it to him. It turned out that he was a lifelong heavy metal fan.

In the early 2000s, Syria's metal scene had a large and passionate following, but just as in Egypt and Lebanon, it was subject to regular crackdowns from the authorities. Although officially a secular state, the country is deeply religious and local bands would rarely announce that they were metal when arranging shows. There were established scenes in Damascus, Latakia and Aleppo, as well as smaller scenes in Homs and Hama, and as internet use became more widespread it was easier for bands to communicate and organise gigs. But they regularly encountered hostility: "It wasn't the authorities, it was the people: they see the word 'metal' and think something bad is going to happen. Like there would be satanic people who are going to rape or kill cats or drink blood or take drugs," Monzer said.

It was public outrage that was behind a government crackdown in 2006, during which Monzer was arrested. "There is no law that says metal music is not allowed or it is prohibited in Syria, but because of the people, the authorities began to arrest metalheads. And then it became a thing: automatically when someone from the government met a metalhead, they would be questioned or held."

The crackdown was provoked by events in Lebanon and soon the familiar pattern kicked off: articles about Syrian satanists began appearing in local newspapers, many of them featuring pictures from the alternative website Deviant Art, including lurid images of young women with crosses in their mouths and pictures of tattoos and piercings. "They used them to say: 'This is how metal people look and this is how they will make your children look. They attack religion.' And they meant physically – they meant we were going to physically attack people," he said.

The crackdown began in Homs and spread to Masyaf, where a popular record store was raided and dozens of CDs and T-shirts burned in the street outside. The store was then shuttered by the authorities. Days later, in Hama, Monzer himself was detained:

I was arrested for satanism. They said: "You are listening to satanic music. You are worshipping the devil. You are involved in dirty sexual acts." They

tried to think of every bad thing they could imagine
and attach it to metal. There were waves of arrests.
It got really bad for metalheads.

The first time Monzer was arrested, the police found a
notebook in which he had written lyrics by Norwegian black
metal band Dimmu Borgir. He was 15 and found himself
having to explain to his interrogators that the irreligious
lyrics were not meant to be taken literally: "I tried to explain
but they wouldn't listen. I had to wait for eight hours in
a small room with my father waiting outside," he said.

But the treatment only made him more determined, more
passionate. "I was really extreme about it because all of that
happened and I knew I wasn't doing anything bad against
anyone. I was just listening to my music. I just wanted to be
in a band and make music and that's it." In the end, Monzer
had to leave his home town of Masyaf and move to another
city, Salamiyah, far from his friends and family. "I had to
live alone just because everybody thought I was a satanist. I
spent three years completely alone, in my house. And during
those years I was just practising and writing articles, getting
more music and metal bands," he said.

While he was in internal exile in his house in
Salamiyah, Monzer became black metal editor of a Syrian
online website – which is how he met Lena, a fellow
metal fan and tattooist in Homs. He wanted her to be an

administrator on the site and eventually they met and fell in love.

A few years earlier, Bashar Haroun was flicking through the channels on TV at home in Aleppo when he came across a video of Metallica's 'The Memory Remains'. He had been a fan of Michael Jackson since his early teens, but this was something completely different. Bashar remembered that the band's style, their black clothes and their dark personas were so different from the pop music that tended to dominate the airwaves. It was serious. "It was the image of the band. The type of music, the power and the energy. The anger. The ideas they had. This wasn't 'Hit Me Baby One More Time', it was deeper," he said. "From this moment I knew that this would be part of my future. I went to the music store and bought the cassette and then started the chase: one band after another, one genre after another. But Metallica's album, *Reload*, it was my first."

Being young and wanting to rebel had a lot to do with it, but as he grew up, Metallica and the other bands that he sought out never lost their importance. "I needed to be different when I was a teenager, but that didn't mean when I grew up I didn't need it anymore – it was the opposite. It is part of my personality and I live it, in every moment of my life," he said.

By 1998, the scene in Aleppo was growing. Damascus was the bigger city and Homs also had an established scene, but Aleppo was its heart. "In Damascus there were a lot of people who believed in metal but in Aleppo there were a lot of people who *played* metal – real musicians were from Aleppo, and real metalheads were from Damascus. That was how it was," Bashar said.

Aside from sporadic harassment by the police, the biggest problem for bands in Aleppo was making live shows break even. Typically, bands would need to hire the venue and then all the equipment separately, meaning that shows were extremely expensive to put on. "On 90 per cent of rock and metal concerts you would make a loss," he said. Then there was the fact that Syrian metal fans tended to want to hear covers rather than original material, and as a result few Syrian bands played their own songs.

Bashar formed his first band with some friends and played twice in Damascus and at least ten times in Aleppo. "We were all beginners before. We loved music but we weren't professional in any way," he said. And then, he formed his first serious band, Orion, and began writing his own material.

A year later, he opened U-Ground Studios, the recording venue and hangout that Adel Saflou would attend six years later and where he would form his first band. For Bashar, U-Ground was not only a focal point for the Aleppo scene but the result of years of frustration with producers in the city who were unable to understand how to record heavy metal: "There was no one who knew how to mix metal, with the double bass drums and the growling vocals," he said.

The crackdown that began in 2006 and forced Monzer Darwish to leave his home town spread to Aleppo and inevitably came to Bashar's door at U-Ground. The studio was raided, their equipment and merchandise confiscated, and Bashar was thrown in jail. He was moved around five of Aleppo's nastiest prisons before being released a month later. "The charge they were looking for was something satanic or something political – and I am neither," he said.

Eventually, Bashar appeared in court and was released by the judge, but the damage was done. U-Ground was reopened but the semi-regular shows that Bashar had organised in Aleppo ceased – the city would not see another live metal show until 2010. More generally, the arrests and harassment of metallers across Syria took an axe to what was a burgeoning scene. Bashar said:

> They made metalheads look ugly in front of
> society and everybody was scared to be with them
> – metalheads were scared to be metalheads. They
> made it look like it was something really dangerous.
> You might waste your life, you waste your money.
> They just put us in the darkest place.

Orion also became inactive, and the songs that they had written before 2008 were not recorded until two years later. Their best-known song, 'Of Freedom and Moor', had originally been written about the situation in Palestine, Bashar said, but the crackdown and its aftermath meant that by the time it was recorded in 2010 it was about problems closer to home. It was about Syria. "For freedom through war / We lose our reason and chances no more / We will stand as one / Together and on our own / Nothing but our unity / Nowhere but our home," Bashar screams in the song's chorus.

It is hard to believe today, but Aleppo largely sat out the Syrian revolution until May 2012. It wasn't oblivious to the mass protests and brutal government reaction to them, but it never saw the kind of popular uprising seen in Homs and Hama. An ethnically diverse and commercial hub of some 2.5 million people, Aleppo had even witnessed government-backed pro-Assad rallies as other cities across Syria were ablaze.

But by 2012 things were changing fast. On 22 July, Syrian rebels invaded the city, headed by the FSA and later Jabhat al-Nusra. In a city that for centuries had been home to Christians, Kurds, Shia, Sunni and Alawites, their sectarian narrative forced residents to pick a side. Once Syria's melting pot, Aleppo became synonymous with the country's shattered heart.

For Bashar, the sectarianism was difficult to bear. In 2010, as the authorities turned their attention to quelling the growing protest movement that was spreading across

Syria, Bashar had begun organising shows. Many Syrians were already leaving the country, heading for Lebanon, Turkey or, for those who could afford it, the Gulf. But as the violence increased around Aleppo, Bashar became more and more determined that he would not abandon either the city or the metal scene. He believed that his scene had always transcended the sectarian divide and could continue to do so. "We put a show on every one or two months. It was to encourage people not to fall into violence and just play music and just stay in the spirit of metal and rock music," he said.

During 2010, 2011 and early 2012, the concerts continued. Monzer recalled that, if anything, the metal scene grew alongside the violence. It was ironic that the bands actually had more freedom to perform once the conflict began. "We had the chance to do it without any distractions from the people who used to bother us," he said. Like Bashar, Monzer sensed that what was happening in the Syrian metal scene was important. It showed a different narrative, one of young people from cities and communities across a torn country, united by their black T-shirts and their passion for extreme music – united by the arrests, the beatings, the isolation that pre-dated Syria's war and will outlast it. Monzer said:

> Whenever something is really hard to do, you
> develop this great passion. It wasn't just concerts;

it was something spiritual for me. When you wore a metal T-shirt back then and saw someone else wearing another band T-shirt in the street you would literally become friends – the next day you would be drinking beer together.

As Aleppo became increasingly uninhabitable, Bashar moved to Latakia, the port city on Syria's western coast that even today has been spared much of the devastation of the rest of the country. He opened a new incarnation of U-Ground and immediately began organising gigs.

Then, during the worst of the fighting in his home city, he and Monzer returned to Aleppo to organise a live show, Life Under Siege, on the front line between the Syrian army and the rebels. It would eventually form the basis for Monzer's documentary, although, at the time, Bashar had his own reasons for returning to Aleppo and putting on a gig as if the war wasn't raging around them. He was proud then – as he is now – that during a war that has pitted Syrian against Syrian, not a single member of Syria's heavy metal community that he knew ever picked up a gun.

Syrian metallers came from across the country's religious and cultural divide – Sunni, Shia, Kurdish and Christian – and they remained metallers, even as Aleppo crumbled around them. "I don't know anyone from all the people around me in the music scene – musicians or just metalheads, rockers and music lovers – who has been involved in any action during this war, until this day," said Bashar. "I think the message was clear from the beginning, that we were apart from all this. We didn't care about the problem of ethnicity or religion. We didn't talk politics. It was just about metal. We were just one happy family." The gig was held at a small venue near the front line between the rebels and the Syrian national army and yet just under 100 people showed up and stayed until close to midnight watching the bands, Bashar recalled.

His own band, Orion, performed their song 'Of Freedom and the Moor', as well as a cover of Sepultura's 'Refuse/Resist'. Just outside the cafe was an abandoned, pockmarked car, and four blocks away was the front line. Even between the venue and the neighbourhoods where many of the fans still lived were dozens of checkpoints, and the risk of sniper fire from the derelict high-rise towers that once dominated what was Aleppo's financial district was ever-present.

Like everywhere else in Aleppo, the venue itself, a former cafe, had no electricity or running water and the bands had to rely on a generator to get the amplifiers and lights working. It regularly packed in, interrupting the music. "We had to run the whole gig on a small generator and there was no fuel," Monzer recalled. "All of that, besides the war. Three or four sides were fighting in that area."

The concert was held during the worst bombardment of Aleppo since the beginning of the war, on Christmas Eve 2013. Mere weeks earlier Assad had dropped barrel bombs, improvised weapons created by cramming barrels full of explosives, on the east of the city and the rebels had promised 'revenge' on the regime-held areas of Aleppo. In Monzer's footage, the remaining metal fans in Aleppo are seen hunkered down in bedrooms, playing and recording music even as the shelling can be heard nearby.

In one poignant scene, Bashar guides Monzer round his house in Aleppo and the pair look in disbelief at the remnants of missiles that are scattered across his garden. Outside his front door, people had hung bed sheets between the trees to stop snipers taking pot-shots at the few residents who remained. The footage cuts to Monzer and three other Syrian metallers walking through the shattered streets of what was once a thriving, liberal city. There is an eerie silence as they pick their way through rubble as high as houses, with the spires of mosques and the metal pylons of high-rise buildings protruding from beneath mountains of concrete. "Two years," says one long-haired metaller, looking at the camera and holding up his index and middle finger: "All this in just two years."

Monzer began documenting daily life for Syrian musicians in 2011, including the life of his friends who were caught up in the fighting. He was on the way to interview a black metal musician from a village close to Hama when a suicide bomber struck the marketplace in the centre of town. "He ended up looking for his siblings amongst the bodies. I was almost there. I was five minutes away," Monzer said. His friend and others from the village armed themselves and have been protecting their homes ever since.

It is not something that Monzer can fathom doing, but he understands his friend's decision. "I cannot agree with any sort of fighting for anything. Or even the concept of guns. The idea is unpleasant for me just to think about," he said. At one point during the film, he asks his friend whether he will ever put down his gun and pick up a guitar: "I don't think it is time for guitars," his friend says.

But neither Monzer nor Bashar agreed – for them, the shows were essential. "During these hard times you will die on the inside if you stop doing what you love. We lost our country but to preserve our souls we had to do what we loved," Monzer said.

> It is important during these hard times because this is what keeps you alive. This is how you can dream and be positive. How you can wake up in the morning and say we have something, we have this concert. I think it is hard for other people to see it like this, but for people who were in the middle of it, during the worst times it was something that kept us alive.

The last of Aleppo's metal community had scattered by the beginning of 2014. Bashar relocated to Latakia, where he opened the latest franchise of U-Ground Studios and tried to keep whatever was left of the scene alive in one of the few peaceful enclaves of Syria that remained. He never tried to get to Europe, or even to Beirut or Turkey; in fact by 2016 he was looking at the possibility of getting back to Aleppo rather than joining the 4.5 million Syrians who have fled the country. "I have plans here. I have already paid 15 years of my life; I can't just give it up and travel and start again – in somewhere I don't know. I don't want to leave my country in such a way," he said.

But even in Latakia, Bashar was finding organising gigs harder and harder, especially for extreme bands. He had started organising shows with rock and jazz cover bands instead – anyone who could play. Bashar was left rueing how different life could have been if the Syrian authorities had not carried out the crackdown in the late 2000s, if Syrian conservatives had realised that a bunch of guys making music and headbanging was no threat to their faith or their customs. He is tortured – even now – by what the Aleppo scene could have become:

> The Aleppo scene was big and it was growing. If we could have just done what we wanted we would have been the number one genre of music in Syria,

I assure you. The only problem that stopped the
scene was the refusal, the denial of society and later
from the police. If they had just said 'Go on, show
us your best', we would have had great bands.

As for the war, Bashar saw parallels in how his community
was treated by the authorities and the orgy of sectarian
violence that the country has become.

Syria turned on young men and women like Bashar,
Monzer, Adel and Lena. It excluded them, humiliated them,
cast them out, called them satanists and devil worshippers,
maligned their music and their passion. Bashar said that
Syria was a divided nation long before 2011 and it was that
refusal to accept people's differences that resulted in the
conflict today. Sunni versus Shia, Christians versus Kurds,
what is that if not the hideously extreme logical extension of
the repression that young metallers suffered at the hands of
their neighbours and the authorities? "It had been growing
for years, for decades, this hatred of the other," Bashar said.
"And we musicians suffered from this hatred. So what about
people who belong to the different religions or places or
ideologies? It had to happen because this society has to learn.
They have to choose between living and killing each other."

It was that hatred that made Adel Saflou an atheist when
he was in exile in Beirut. He remembered hearing the imam
of a Sunni mosque giving a Friday sermon about the festival

of Easter. "He was saying not to congratulate Christians on Easter because it was against Islam. He said they were kaffirs [unbelievers]," he recalled. The sermon disgusted Adel not only because it was hateful, but because it was just the kind of language that had been used to justify the years of hate and repression, the beatings and the arrests, that had been meted out if not to him then to his friends. "I thought: this is where the hate starts," he said. "This is where all the terrible shit in my life started."

For Monzer, that hatred did not stop when they left Syria. He moved to Algeria first, where he worked for six months for a graphic design company. When his contract ended, his boss refused to pay him and so he returned to Beirut with nothing. He went to Turkey but in Istanbul found that Turkish landlords would refuse to rent to Syrians; even when Monzer managed to get a friend to help him negotiate, he was allowed to stay for only three months at a time. Given that he had no rental contract, he could not get connected to utilities and had to live without running water.

He noticed a change in attitudes in Turkey towards refugees as right-wing anti-Syrian parties grew in popularity. In his neighbourhood in Istanbul he would see racist graffiti every day. "It wasn't the perfect environment to think about starting again – this is when I decided to go to Europe," he said.

Lena, who had been living in Latakia, met Monzer in Turkey and they began preparing to make the crossing to

Greece with the people-smuggling gangs who openly ply their trade on the streets of Istanbul. Monzer and Lena, who had had little exposure to the world of organised crime during their lives in Syria, were suddenly thrust into a world of shady characters and dodgy dealings, but it was their only hope of starting again. "You're in survivor mode. You have this huge dream in your head. I think this is what moved me. I thought that when I finally arrived in Europe things would be positive again That life would be fair with me for once," said Monzer.

A few weeks later they packed into a flimsy rubber dinghy with four dozen other desperate Syrians and crossed the Mediterranean. On the beach, the smugglers ordered the couple to sit on opposite sides of the boat, so, as they were thrown around in the open sea, they could not even see each other. When they finally reached Greece, they remained on the beach, helping the other refugees register with the Greek authorities. They were still dressed in their waterproof clothes and coats and looked like the other Syrians who had made the perilous crossing. They walked with the families and others who they had helped to the camp, where they changed into their regular clothes. It was then that the friendliness of their fellow refugees evaporated. "When they saw Lena wearing shorts they said we were infidels and they stopped talking to us," Monzer said. "This is the first thing that happened to me in Europe."

The discrimination that he and Lena had faced in Syria

had followed them to Greece – they were refugees not just in Europe but among their own people.

It followed them again to Holland, where they flew after buying fake Spanish passports in Athens. As part of their asylum process, they were expected to attend classes to help them adjust to life in Europe. When they went to the university, they found themselves surrounded by conservative families similar to those they had met on the beach in Greece. Monzer almost came to blows with a man in one session who argued that it wasn't right for women to be educated, as Lena sat a few desks away.

In other classes, Monzer said that Dutch tutors would caution him that in Holland it was not acceptable to beat your wife – as if he ever had, or ever would. Monzer said:

You ask yourself: "Why have we risked our lives?"
Because we almost drowned in the Mediterranean.
It was terrifying. And after all that, when you end
up in the place you have always dreamed about,
everyone thinks that you're violent or that you are
not tolerant or that you beat your wife. That you're
a radical, or you're ignorant, or you have never
seen the TV or the internet. All of that combined:
it doesn't help you stay the happy person you were
once. In the middle of the war I was more positive
than I am today.

Holed up in their flat in Oosthuizen, Monzer and Lena seem almost nostalgic for Syria, even in the early days of the war. Monzer speaks of his home town – of the restaurants and the bars on the three mountains that surround it, of the cafes that are always open and the shops that never close. Of the warmth and the friendliness of the people there. He and Lena are grateful for the sanctuary that Europe has given them, but despite everything Syria burns brightly in their hearts:

> We dream of going back. We talk about going back every day if things get better. Whenever we call someone and tell them, they are like, no you're crazy, why would you leave safety and all of that to get back? But I think it is about the small details: it is about your neighbours, and your friends. It's about being in a friendly environment. Everything else you can get used to: new places, new views, new streets – these are objects. But when it comes to actions, the way people see you. You start thinking: "Have I done the right thing? Have I risked my life for the right thing?"

When he thinks about returning, the one thing that crosses his mind is whether things would be different. In the early days of the war, Bashar and Monzer could arrange shows in Latakia and Aleppo and nobody seemed to care. Would the arrests and the accusations be a thing of the past in the new Syria?

The thought is a tantalising one for Monzer and Lena, sitting on their battered couch in an empty room, watching footage from Syria and another lifetime. "One day, can we get back – all of us – and do our thing? Will they accept us? Because here we can do whatever the hell we want. If we get back and wanted to do something, a concert, and we weren't accepted, that would be a huge disappointment," he said.

* * *

As Adel sat amidst the chaos of the boat listening to 'Somewhere Over the Rainbow', the thought crossed his mind that this was how it would end. During 2015, 3,771 migrants drowned in the Mediterranean and there was no good reason why he wouldn't be number 3,772.

It was dark, around 2 am, when he managed to get hold of the coastguard and they said help was on its way, but it was another six hours before they heard the whirring of the helicopter above their heads. They were rescued in small groups before being taken to Samos and then to Athens, from where Adel and his cousins walked to Austria via Macedonia, Serbia and Hungary.

In Almelo, Holland, Adel was living in a single room in an asylum centre on the outskirts of the town, surrounded by green fields and cows and quaint little Dutch houses. The centre was a shabby selection of prefabricated two-storey buildings, and Adel's neighbours, mostly Syrian families, eyed him curiously with his piercings and tattoos – but it was safe and warm and he could come and go as he pleased.

Since first arriving in Holland, he had seen the inside of nine different asylum centres, one of which was a maximum security prison. His cousins have been housed elsewhere in Holland and he sees them from time to time. When he looks at them sitting together with their kids running around, oblivious, he remembers how he strapped on their life jackets on the beach in Izmir and wondered whether they would survive the night. "I don't know how we made it. I look at my cousins now and think: 'How can we do that? How can we joke about it now?'" he said. "I don't believe in miracles but it was. It was a miracle of human deed."

Adel had spent the first two years of his life as a refugee in Lebanon, first near Tripoli, north of Beirut, where he studied mass communication at university before being kicked out for possession of cannabis. He was jailed for a month and the government took away his student resident's permit. Like many Syrians who had crossed the border to Lebanon, he melted into the huge refugee population in Beirut.

By the summer of 2016, the city was packed with refugees, many of whom would beg for change from the expatriates and wealthy Lebanese who frequented the bars and cafes of Gemmayzeh, in the city's Christian east.

In Bekaa, the fertile valley that joins Lebanon and Syria, every vacant patch of land was taken up with tents as tens of thousands of Syrians eked out a meagre existence working in farming or construction.

Lebanese workers were frustrated with the hundreds of thousands of Syrians who had made Lebanon their home since 2012, believing that the influx of cheap labour was hitting their jobs and salaries. The Lebanese government, which closed the border in 2015, had begun arresting Syrians who were not permitted to be in the country, and while there were no reports of refugees actually being deported – which would be in contravention of Lebanon's international obligations – conditions were deteriorating.

Adel was sent money regularly by his father, who lives in the UK, and relied on a support network of friends and musicians from Aleppo and elsewhere in Syria – so he fared better than most. "I laid low for like a year and a half. I just sat there and recorded an album," he said. It was recorded under the name of Adel's solo project, Ambrotype, and was a concept based, appropriately, on the tyrannical rule of an immortal despot. It dealt with Syria, his home, and drew on his proximity to Syrian musicians and bands that he still hung out with in Beirut.

But by 2016 the music already felt outdated. His voyage from Aleppo to Beirut, from Izmir to Samos, from Athens through Macedonia, Hungary and Austria and now to

Holland has changed him as a person and as a musician. Adel's music is no longer about Syria – about his old life, a world that no longer exists and maybe never will again; it is about exile. "I am not what I was a year ago, not even close. I have a different view on life. I don't know what I am. I am lost," he said.

Sitting in his tiny room in Almelo, Adel is tormented by the fact that, even if he and his friends are able to start again in Europe, thousands of miles from home, what they had is gone forever. He thinks about how it was once so different. He remembers how, after a show in Aleppo, the bands and their friends would head back to someone's house with a load of beers. They would get drunk and smoke cigarettes. They would reminisce and they would talk until dawn, when light would seep through the curtains and everyone would make their way home. "It was the best time of my life," he said.

But that crowd is scattered now, in towns and cities and refugee camps across Europe and the Middle East. Their friends and relatives dead, their homes destroyed. "Everyone that I know is fucked up. Everyone I knew," he said. "Every person I loved is deeply scarred."

* * *

France was home to tens of thousands of Syrians by 2017. The country had initially basked in warmth and welcome for refugees from that shattered nation, but times were changing. The Paris attacks of November 2015 marked a change of narrative in Europe, with those on the right arguing that France should begin turning away those who fled Syria. Yasser arrived in Paris in 2013, during a different era, and he had been shocked at how attitudes had changed. He drew parallels with the anti-immigrant racism of the 1960s: "It is like we have gone back 50 years," he said.

He knew that he was lucky to have got out when he did. Muhammed, their Syrian bandmate, is back in Yarmouk having failed to secure asylum. Ahmad Razouk made it to Europe only to be deported with his wife and child back to Algeria, a country he had left when he was two years old.

In April 2015, extremist rebel factions seized 60 per cent of Yarmouk and then in July typhoid spread among the 18,000 residents who remained. When the UN released an image of tens of thousands of residents squeezed between rows of crumbling buildings, queuing for food, Yarmouk became yet another icon of the death and destruction of Syria's civil war. As well as the regular outbreaks of violence between rebel groups and Palestinian factions, Assad relentlessly bombed the camp as he tried to stop the rebels from reaching Damascus. Even if the war were to end tomorrow, Yarmouk would never be the same.

But it is France, not Syria, that is Yasser's home now. He was born a refugee, and he remains one. As a Palestinian he never had nationality in Syria: the country was a refugee camp for him then, as France is to him now. Like millions of other Palestinians who have never set foot in their homeland, he dreams of return but accepts that he may never have that chance. "Coming to France has taught me that the place where I am, this is my country," he said.

Yasser recently met a French girl and visited her home town to meet her parents. He had his brother, a circle of friends and fellow musicians, a job and a home. Life was really just beginning for Yasser. He had once ridden his bike down the middle of a bombed-out street in Yarmouk, war raging all around him, to rescue the songs he now plays to tens of thousands of people. He had been lucky that day, just as he and Mohammed had been lucky to reach Europe when so many others didn't. But they had fought hard for the rest, they had to. Yasser and Mohammed had nothing to go back to, they could only go forward.

EPILOGUE

NO MATTER HOW ROUGH THE WAVES MAY BE,

TOGETHER, WITH RESOLUTION

AND PERSEVERANCE,

WE WILL MAKE THE CROSSING.

--AHMED FOUAD NEGM

n May 2016 a handful of friends gathered in the front room of Ramy Essam's apartment in Malmo to celebrate his birthday. Five years earlier Ramy had been labelled the voice of Tahrir Square. In 2011 he had stood on stage in Tahrir and, at 23 years old, had played in front of crowds that even The Rolling Stones or Metallica would struggle to pull in. But few of the people in the tiny room on the third floor of a block of council flats in this Swedish city had known him then.

It had been three years since I first met Ramy in Cairo's Zamalek in 2013 and watched him play to a few dozen Egyptians sat on chairs outside the Goethe Institute. The coup that would unseat Mohammed Morsi as president was weeks away and Egypt was tired. Tahrir was littered with blast walls and debris; riot police stood menacingly behind barbed wire and surrounded by a thick carpet of stones, thrown by the few hard-core protesters who remained.

The revolutionary graffiti, the ragged tents and the ripped flags were still there. But the riots that had engulfed

Cairo a couple of weeks earlier had waned and the crowds that gathered could be counted in their dozens. Ordinary Egyptians seemed to think of Tahrir as an annoyance. On my way in from the airport, I saw a car driving against the flow of traffic on the elevated highway that snakes through Cairo. "This is what I am talking about," said my driver, "since the revolution everybody just does whatever they want."

Malmo could not have been more different, with its neat buildings and orderly streets. As the evening progressed and the ragtag bunch of expatriates, writers and musicians got steadily drunk, word went around that Ramy was going to perform. He squatted against the wall with his guitar and began to play protest songs from Cairo – from another era, another lifetime. The two dozen or so people in the apartment perched on chairs or sat on the floor as Ramy strummed in his rough, flamenco style and rasped his lyrics in tough Egyptian street Arabic. A few minutes in, he performed a slower song – a new one – and a young woman began singing along in a beautiful, haunting counterpoint.

My mind drifted back to Cairo. I remembered how in 2011 I had watched the *shabab* (the youth) with brooms, frantically brushing the rainwater into the gutters in an ultimately futile effort to protect their revolutionary camp from the elements. How I had walked across the Qasr el-Nile bridge on a cold evening when debris littered the streets and was asked for my ID at a checkpoint run by the revolutionaries at the entrance to Tahrir. One of them patted me down and, when I produced a British passport, smiled. "You are welcome," he said and waved me into that magical square where so much had been achieved, and so much had been lost.

That year, Ramy had played his songs and hundreds of thousands had sung along. Now he leaned against the living room wall and played those same songs to us in the warm Malmo night.

When Ramy finished, Mai opened a laptop and played a video she had compiled of friends in Egypt wishing him happy birthday, one by one. Most people didn't know who most of the faces were, and, as it went on, the crowd drifted away. Drinks were poured, conversations started, cigarettes lit. But Ramy sat close to the screen with a huge grin. Behind the messages were the sounds of the traffic, the bustle, the chants – the addictive chaos of Cairo.

I was reminded of something Ramy had said earlier that day, when we sat on the second floor of the theatre where he performed in downtown Malmo. As the sun streaked through the dirty windows onto the wooden floor, I asked why he wanted to go back to Egypt, knowing that he would be arrested and probably jailed. In this era when tens of thousands risk their lives crossing the deserts and seas to reach Europe, this hallowed land, he has what so many want: a way out, a family, a new life in a country where you

can say what you want to say and be who you want to be.
Yet still he looks to Egypt. "I miss everything – *everything*,"
he said, smiling and sucking the air through his teeth.

> I miss my family and my friends. The streets, the
> vibe, the people, the revolution. The struggle. It
> looks bad. It looks miserable and hopeless. Even
> my close friends, they say: "How can you be
> optimistic like that?" But during the revolution I
> made a deal with myself – that I can't lose hope,
> because losing hope in this struggle is a betrayal.
> I can't live with myself if I betray the revolution or
> my friends who died.

A couple of months later, I took a long bus ride through
the green fields of northern Holland to see Monzer and
Lena in the small town where they had lived since being
granted asylum.

Oosthuizen is close to the tourist village of Edam, and
surrounded by farms and canals and grey-haired tourists
taking pictures and buying cheese. Monzer showed me
pictures of their makeshift camps in Greece, their sleeping
bags on rough grass, surrounded by trash. He seemed
ashamed of the way the pair had lived during those dark
months walking across Europe, sleeping in train stations,
shabby hotels and often just by the side of the road.

We spent the afternoon in their empty flat, drinking tea and watching the rough edit of Monzer's film – *Syrian Metal Is War*. As we watched footage of downtown Homs, the spires of mosques collapsed across once busy thoroughfares, overturned buses and mountains of rubble, the couple pointed out streets that they remembered. This was the city where Lena grew up, that Monzer knew well. It is where they had walked with their tattoos and long hair. It was where they had played gigs and hung out in cafes. It was home – and now it was gone.

As the sun dipped lower in the sky, Monzer began to describe his home village, Masyaf. He described how it was set between three mountains and how in the evenings the hills came alive with the twinkling lights of the cafes and restaurants dotted between the trees. "You know everybody. It doesn't really sleep. You can always walk and there is always something moving. Shops never close, supermarkets never close," he said.

Both he and Lena were careful to stress that they were grateful for the sanctuary that Holland has provided them, when so many more are trapped amidst the war or lost in camps in Turkey, Jordan or Lebanon. But the picturesque little Dutch towns will never be able to replace Masyaf or Homs, Aleppo or Damascus. Monzer and Lena have little to do here but watch TV and talk, and when they talk they think of all the things they never got to do in Syria before they left. The cities they didn't visit, the historic and beautiful locations they never saw.

They torment themselves with these memories and when, homesick, they call friends and families in Latakia or Beirut, they are told they are crazy: they should be happy. They are told to start a new life, to forget about Syria. But they can't.

The following day in Almelo, Holland, Adel Saflou showed me around the apartment he shared with two other refugee families. His room contained nothing but a laptop, a single bed and a guitar, donated to him by a friend. He had started performing again at the local community centre and he was relatively close to Amsterdam when he wanted a change of scene.

But his friends were scattered: Bashar in Latakia, many others in Beirut. His mother in Turkey, his other family applying for asylum in Britain. Adel had wanted to leave Idlib before the war made it essential: he didn't see a future for a guy like him, who looked different, thought different, wanted more. He had tried Beirut and, when that didn't work out, he tried Europe.

But Adel has experienced more pain in his 23 years than most of us will see in a lifetime. When we met in Almelo he seemed restless, as if that year crossing Europe, almost dying, sleeping rough, was still ringing in his ears. His story poured out over hours as we sat outside a twee little cafe on

Almelo high street. Just metres away was a bustling artisan street market, where well-dressed locals and their families shopped for high-end coffee and homemade jam.

The Dutch had made him feel welcome and, like Monzer, he felt compelled to tell me more than once that he didn't take his sanctuary for granted. But he still wrestled with the descent into madness and bloodshed that had swept his country in just five years.

During the day we spent together, the only time the darkness lifted from Adel's eyes was when we swapped stories about Opeth, or Katatonia, the shows we had seen and the ones we still wanted to see. Months later he shared a selfie on Facebook from an Opeth gig in Amsterdam. He was right up front, against the barrier, with the devil horns raised and his mouth open in an almighty roar. The fans around him looked bemused but, of course, how could they have understood how far Adel had travelled to get there?

As for Mohammed and Yasser Jamous, as I finished this book Refugees of Rap were rising stars. Yasser's French was almost fluent and the pair was touring Europe. They had turned their incredibly difficult voyage into music, and hundreds of thousands of people, whether they were displaced or second, third or fourth generation Arabs, were finding solace in their songs. They were connecting.

At one point, just after midnight, as we walked the streets of Paris' thirteenth arrondissement back in the summer of 2016, I asked Yasser how he had felt about the terrorist attacks a year earlier, when ISIS gunmen brought carnage to the streets of the French capital. It was a clumsy question that I immediately regretted, with the implication that he would have something to say as a Muslim, a refugee and a Syrian living in Paris. But he began telling me how he had been at work and when he heard the news had immediately called Mohammed. He had rung again and again, but his brother didn't answer. He began to panic, calling other friends, to see if anyone had seen him. Finally, Mohammed answered: he had been asleep.

His story is the same as that of many others that day – of desperate calls to friends and relatives, of anger, sadness and eventually relief – for the lucky ones. It was not the fact that he nominally shares a religion with the people who brought such wanton bloodshed to the streets of Paris – as well as to Brussels, Baghdad, Kabul and Beirut – that was important; Yasser chose not to answer the question as a Syrian, or a Muslim, but as a brother. In these times, when we turn on each other because of our faith or our country of birth, I like to remember Yasser's story and the fact that, above all, we are brothers and sisters, fathers and mothers, lovers and friends.

I wrote *Rock in a Hard Place* during a period of intense change. On 23 June 2016, Britain voted to leave the European Union and ignited a tide of hatred and racism that surprised many of us who are proud of Britain's inclusivity. As I was travelling around Europe and the Middle East, talking to people who were strangers in their own countries due to the way they dressed, the music they played and the things they wanted, I felt more and more like a stranger in my own. Britain turned on its minorities, its minorities turned on each other, and our leaders began publicly maligning the notion of global citizenship – the idea that we have more in common than we have that divides us. We became staggeringly hard-hearted towards people who could have been Ramy, or Adel, or Monzer and Lena, or Sherine, or Meraj and Anahid: people who had fled hardship and had come to Europe to seek a new life.

While hearing and transcribing and writing the stories that make up this book, I was, like everyone else, following the bitter fight for the US presidency, which, in November 2016, Donald Trump would win. Like so many others who consider themselves internationalists, Trump's divisive and racist narrative was anathema to me.

As I watched it triumph, I was struck by something that Tamer Nafar from DAM had told me earlier that year. He said that he had been watching the coverage of the funeral of Shimon Peres on television and he had heard Barack Obama compare the late Israeli leader to Nelson Mandela. It struck him then that the world has accepted Israel's treatment of the Palestinians – they just want Israel not to treat them so badly that it is obvious. As hopes for a Palestinian state became more and more futile, as ISIS raged in Iraq, as revolutions were buried in Egypt and Syria, he couldn't help but feel that the Middle East was doomed. "To be honest, I think we lost," he said. "I think the Arabs lost."

The world has been hard on the characters in this book. Iranian rapper Erfan Paydar told us about his treatment after 9/11, when he was thrown in jail simply because he was born in Iran. Eslam Jawaad, the Syrian-Lebanese rapper, had similar experiences after the 7 July attack in London in 2005 when he was racially abused by immigration staff and detained at Heathrow Airport when he arrived on tour with Gorillaz. "Post 9/11, shit changed," he said. "It was a crazy period to be in the West."

Eslam's songs are unashamedly political: anti-Zionist, anti-war. He sees a direct correlation between that and his treatment by the authorities: "I think Arab rappers who have something to say are sort of between a rock and a hard place in that they are not fully free to express what they want in their home countries, nor are they fully free to express what they want in the West." He wrote a song, 'Criminals', about it: "It's about how it is fine to sing about pimping and drug dealing and as soon as you start talking about political shit you actually get treated like a criminal," he said.

In early 2017 it wasn't only Arab musicians that were treated like criminals. President Trump made good on his campaign promise and banned entry to nationals of seven Muslim-majority countries: Iraq, Syria, Somalia, Sudan, Iran, Libya and Yemen. Newspapers worldwide carried harrowing reports of Iraqis and Iranians being detained at US airports and quizzed on their religious beliefs or whether they loved America. The ban was struck down by the US courts but a few weeks later was reinstated, this time with an exception for Iraqi nationals.

There was less furore the second time around. There were fewer protests, fewer horror stories about families torn apart and fewer thundering opinion pieces about America's democratic decline. Perhaps the world was getting used to the Trump era. I listened to pundits criticising not the ethics of the ban itself but rather the chaotic way it had been handled by the White House. It felt as if we had reached a perverse new normal: where a country once proud to give sanctuary to the tired, poor and hungry was turning people away based on the lottery of birth.

While that all played out over the Atlantic, right-wing populist Geert Wilders' hateful rhetoric about Muslims was winning him support in the Netherlands, a country once known as the liberal bastion of Europe. In France, anti-immigration National Front leader Marine Le Pen was poised to win the first round of the French elections. Across Europe, far right movements who once existed on the fringes were emboldened.

I recalled the early days of the 2015 migrant crisis, when tens of thousands of Syrian and African refugees crossed the Mediterranean. Back then, British football fans had held 'Refugees Welcome' banners in the terraces. British families had offered spare bedrooms to Syrian families. A cartoon in a British newspaper that showed migrants entering Europe with rats running around their feet drew comparisons to Nazi propaganda and was roundly condemned. Even amongst those who were wary of immigration or critical of multiculturalism there seemed to be a consensus that Syrians or Iraqis or Africans fleeing war, violence and poverty should be given shelter in Europe.

It took barely a year for that attitude to change. When the children of Calais refugee camp first began to arrive in the UK in October 2016, mainstream British newspapers ran inflammatory articles questioning their true ages. Editors ran images of refugees smirking and laughing, as if they had got one over on the British state. By early 2017 the pulse of the nation was such that when the Home Office suddenly reneged on its decision to resettle thousands more Calais children, it didn't even feel the need to explain why. It was emblematic of our new normal: of the insular, nationalistic Britain that we had become.

As I finished this book, I couldn't help but reflect how alien that narrative felt. We were constantly being told that people from other places were different, that they had different religions and different values. Trump and his acolytes were urging us to live as islands, to lock our doors and put bars on our windows and divide the world into friends and enemies according to race or religion. Well, heavy metal had always been the closest thing I had to a religion, and over two decades in a dozen countries it had only bridged islands and opened doors. It had taught me the most valuable lesson I have ever learned, that there is a lot more that unites than divides us.

* * *

In 2011, as Cairo raged with protests and chaos was all around us, I met Sameh Sabry for the first time. We arranged to meet at a bank where he was working. The doors were boarded up to avoid it being looted – others had been in recent months – and we sat in the cafeteria and talked about metal as his colleagues milled around in smart suits. The bank had been closed for weeks and so we stood drinking our coffee at the desks that once would have been used to serve customers. I was a stranger and we were both guarded when we talked politics, but as our conversation shifted to music we both relaxed. It was no longer a journalist talking to a source but two men talking about bands.

In 2013, after Morsi had taken power, we met again in Zamalek and Cairo was a different place. Things were looking bad for Egypt and Sameh's early optimism had faded. He left Egypt for Dubai a few months later.

We kept in touch over the years and in 2016 we spoke at the tail end of my writing this book. We talked for over an hour and, at the very end, he said something that finally nailed what had brought him, me, everyone else together.

He told me how, as kids, he and his friends would swap mix tapes so much that the constant use would make them unlistenable. He talked about how, when they were first learning English, they would write down the lyrics and then fight about what they meant. They'd be spitting at each other and fighting and then they'd finally agree and go and sit down and have a coffee and a beer.

Those days are long behind Sameh, as they are behind many of those who are quoted in this book, whether because they have been forced to leave or they have chosen to. But the fire remains.

Sameh was recently in Thailand on business, and the first thing he did was the first thing he always does when he travels – he found a rock club. He took a seat at the bar and looked around. Sitting at the other tables and on the dance floor were Thais, Brits, Americans, Africans, Arabs and Australians. There were men and women. There were old people and young people, fat people and skinny people. All with their own stories, their own values, their lives and loves and scars.

At some point in time, all these people had found something in heavy metal music. It could have been Journey or Sepultura, Burzum or Guns N' Roses. It could have been on a battered old cassette or on YouTube. But after they had heard it, their lives had changed forever. "I was seven hours away from Dubai, 11 hours from my homeland, surrounded by these people. We're all in one bar, in the middle of Phuket, having a beer, shouting and screaming our lungs out for a live band," he said. "That's it. As God is my witness, the moment I stepped in the door, I felt home."

ACKNOWLEDGEMENTS

This book has been in the making for a number of years and it is difficult for me to even begin to fathom the amount of people that have helped make it possible. I owe an immense debt of gratitude to my friends in the music scene across the Middle East, both those who made it into *Rock in a Hard Place* and many others who I had to leave out. My first acknowledgement is to all of them: to the tribe. I can't thank you enough for welcoming me into your countries, your homes and your shows and treating me like a brother.

I would particularly like to thank: Ramy Essam, Fawaz, Ahmed, Cherine Amr, Lydia Canaan, Meraj and Anahid, Dahaaka from Hatecrowned and Filthy Fuck from Ayat; Hasan Hatrash, Sameh Sabry and Noor Hamed; Federico Gomez, Ashmedi and Ishay Berger; Bashar Haroun, Adel Saflou, Monzer Darwish and Muhammed Saad.

I regret that I didn't have the space or the time to cover the many other thriving metal and hip hop scenes in the Middle East, including in Morocco, Bahrain, Jordan and Tunisia. All I can say is that there are many brave musicians making incredible music across the Middle East and I hope that for readers this book serves as a primer, not an exhaustive account of all of them. I must make special mention of my friends from Jordan – Muhammed Jaber, Rak Hiasat and Fares Sweidan – who have helped me with this book despite my difficult decision not to cover the Jordanian scene. As promised, if there is ever a Volume II of *Rock in a Hard Place*, Chalice of Doom will be in it.

Many of the stories in this book began as profiles and features for other magazines, including *Delayed Gratification* and the Middle East editions of *Rolling Stone* and *Esquire*. I was lucky to have understanding editors at these titles who pushed (and paid) me to pursue what would otherwise have been a labour of love. In particular I would like to thank *Esquire Middle East* editor-in-chief Jeremy Lawrence, who commissioned the 2010 story from Saudi Arabia that gave this book its name.

I also want to thank Karl Baz, George Durzi, Dayal Patterson, Hugh Lovatt, John Davison, Chris Leamy and anyone else who gave me advice, contacts or a place to sleep over the past 12 months. My father-in-law, Tony Elfer, was an early supporter of this project, as were my parents, Simon Crowcroft and Imogen Nicholls. My brother Barnaby was a dedicated editor whose suggestions improved the manuscript immeasurably.

It has been a pleasure to work with Kika Sroka-Miller and the team at Zed, and I must also thank my copyeditor, Judith Forshaw. Any errors and omissions are of course my own.

And finally to my wife, best friend and partner on so many adventures, Helen, without whom this book would never have been written.

FURTHER LISTENING
AND READING

One of the pleasures of writing this book has been the opportunity to listen to so much great music, not just by the bands included in *Rock in a Hard Place* but by the artists who have inspired them.

It has been 20 years since I first got *Appetite for Destruction* by Guns N' Roses on cassette and fell down the rock 'n' roll rabbit hole. I've spent many thousands of happy hours down there since and I like to imagine that this book will go even a small way to helping others do the same.

The list below is by no means exhaustive, but I hope that those readers who may not be grounded in heavy metal, punk or hip hop may find it useful.

al-Namrood, *Diaji al-Joor* (2015)

Anaal Nathrakh, *Vanitas* (2012)

Ayat, *Six Years of Dormant Hatred* (2008)

Bathory, *Under the Sign of the Black Mark* (1987)

Blaakyum, *Line of Fear* (2016)

Burzum, *Filosofem* (1996), *Belus* (2010)

Carcass, *Heartwork* (1993)

Confess, *Confess* (2016)

Crass, *The Feeding of the Five Thousand* (1978)

Creative Waste, *Slaves to Conformity* (2012)

DAM, *Dabke on the Moon* (2012)

Damaar, *Triumph Through Spears of Sacrilege* (2007)

Dark Philosophy, *50,000 Years* (2011)

Darkthrone, *A Blaze in the Northern Sky* (1992)

Dead Kennedys, *Fresh Fruit for Rotting Vegetables* (1980)

Dead Prez, *Let's Get Free* (2000)

Drudkh, *Blood in Our Wells* (2006)

Eminem, *The Eminem Show* (2002)

From the Vastland, *Chamrosh* (2016)

Gorgoroth, *Ad Majorem Sathanas Gloriam* (2006)

Grieving Age, *Merely the Fleshless We and the Awed* (2013)

Hatecrowned, *Newborn Serpent* (2015)

Immortal, *Sons of Northern Darkness* (2002)

Iron Monkey, *Our Problem* (1997)

Katatonia, *Brave Murder Day* (1996), *The Great Cold Distance* (2006)

Malikah, *Ya #7akakeen* (2014)

Massive Scar Era, *Comes Around You* (2012)

Mayhem, *De Mysteriis Dom Sathanas* (1994)

Melechesh, *Enki* (2015)

Metallica, *Master of Puppets* (1986)

Mgla, *Exercises in Futility* (2015)

Nader Sadek, *In the Flesh* (2011)

Ramy Essam, *Songs from a Stolen Spring* (2014)

Refugees of Rap, *Haram* (2013)

Scarab, *Blinding the Masses* (2010), *Serpents of the Nile* (2015)

Sepultura, *Arise* (1991), *Roots* (1996)

Soap Kills, *The Best of Soap Kills* (2015)

System Ali, *System Ali* (2013)

Taake, *Noregs Vaapen* (2011), *Stridens Hus* (2014)

Venom, *Black Metal* (1982)

Wolves in the Throne Room, *Black Cascade* (2009)

Yellow Dogs, *Upper Class Complexity* (2012)

A number of books have been helpful to me for the political and musical sections of this book.

Beirut, Samir Kassir (2010)

Pity the Nation: Lebanon at War, Robert Fisk (2001)

A Revolution Undone: Egypt's Road Beyond Revolt, H. A. Hellyer (2016)

Cairo: My City, Our Revolution, Ahdaf Soueif (2012)

The Egyptians: A Radical Story, Jack Shenker (2016)

Last of the Giants: The True Story of Guns N' Roses, Mick Wall (2016)

Lords of Chaos: The Bloody Rise of the Satanic Metal Underground, Michael Moynihan and Didrik Søderlind (1998)

Heavy Metal Islam, Mark LeVine (2008)

Black Metal: Evolution of the Cult, Dayal Patterson (2013)

Inside the Kingdom, Robert Lacey (2010)

ABOUT THE AUTHOR

Orlando Crowcroft has spent over a decade as a journalist and foreign correspondent based in London, Shanghai, Dubai and Jerusalem.